# Robert Winston

# It's Elementary!

DK

**DK**

LONDON, NEW YORK, MUNICH,
MELBOURNE, AND DELHI

**Senior editors** Deborah Lock, Elinor Greenwood
**Designed by** Claire Patané, Karen Hood,
Clare Harris, Sadie Thomas, Poppy Joslin
**Publishing manager** Susan Leonard
**Picture researcher** Liz Moore
**Production** Sarah Jenkins
**DTP designer** Ben Hung
**Indexer** Chris Bernstein
**Jacket designer** Hedi Gutt
**Jacket editor** Mariza O'Keeffe
**Jacket copywriter** Adam Powley
**US Editor** Margaret Parrish

**Consultant** Peter Morris,
the Science Museum, London

First published in United States in 2007 by DK Publishing
375 Hudson Street, New York, New York 10014

07 08 09 10 11 10 9 8 7 6 5 4 3 2 1
WD142 - 05/07

Foreword copyright © 2007 Robert Winston
Copyright © 2007 Dorling Kindersley Limited

DK books are available at special discounts when purchased in bulk for
sales promotions, premiums, fundraising, or educational use. For details, contact:
DK Publishing Special Markets
375 Hudson Street, New York, New York 10014
Special Sales@dk.com

A catalog record for this book is available from the Library of Congress.

ISBN: 978-0-7566-2666-2

Color reproduction by GRB Editrice, Italy
Printed and bound in Italy by L.E.G.O.

Discover more at
**www.dk.com**

"The elements are the be all and end all of everything. They provide the answers to many of life's burning questions: What are we made of? What keeps us alive? They also help us to understand such things as how to reduce our carbon footprint, and how to make a car run with the only emission being water.

The quest for answers about the world, the universe, and everything in it, began a long time ago, and still there is so much to know. Out of the dark mystery of the gold-seeking alchemists emerged something pure—knowledge of the elements.

Inventors know and understand the elements and how we use the elements changes all the time— as new properties are found or harnessed, suddenly a humble lightbulb turns into an energy-efficient, automatic downlighter.

As a doctor, I have certainly been very glad to know about the elements. But it is also nice to know what I am slipping on as I ski down a mountain, what makes a television work, and that the blood of spiders, octopus, and snails is blue because it's full of copper!

All this and more is the subject of this fun and fascinating book. The study of the elements has unraveled the mysteries of the universe, and provided some great stories along the way. So let's go ele-MENTAL!"

ROBERT WINSTON

Hg

# CONTENTS

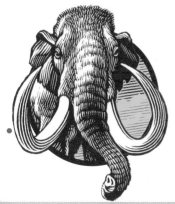

**"ELEMENTS** are *everywhere* and *make everything.* If *you* break down *anything* to its basic *building* blocks, all you will find are *elements, and nothing else*. There are about **100 elements** altogether but most things are made up of only a few.

You are reading *words* in *printer's ink,* made from the element CARBON. The paper is composed of CARBON, HYDROGEN, and OXYGEN. Some 25 *elements* go into making *you.* From the Sun in the sky to the *universe* beyond, EVERYTHING is ELEMENTS.

An *element is the simplest substance of anything and everything.*

# In the BEGINNING

" Elements have been a part of human life since... well, since life, or, in fact, anything, began.

When we first started out as early humans, we found them really handy. We could make clubs out of bones, tools out of stones, and melt gold to make beautiful bowls.

*We were really getting somewhere, but where?*

With all our bashing, shaping, and heating, we had no idea we were conducting the earliest experiments on the elements.

It took several ages before those very smart people, the ancient Greeks, came along to shed some light on things... "

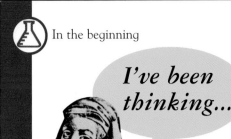

*I've been thinking...*

Empedocles

# GREEK *geeks*

**The great thinkers** of ancient Greece turned their attention to *finding* out exactly what **EVERYTHING** is made of.

## *Earth*

*Everything with dry, cold properties was seen as the earth element.*

## *Water*

*Everything wet and cold was of the water element.*

## *Fire*

*Everything with hot, dry properties was of the fire element.*

# 490 BCE – 430 BCE

## *Shape up!*

The great thinker Plato jumped on the bandwagon by suggesting that the atoms of each element were a different shape. It just so happens there are five regular 3-D shapes—and these seemed to fit well with the five elements.

Cubes are satisfyingly earthlike since they can stack together leaving no gaps.

This rounded, ball-like shape was chosen to represent a flowing water atom.

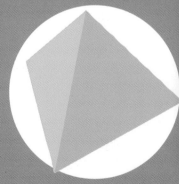

Plato thought a spiked shape would fit fire, since fire felt sharp when it burned.

# ATOM means *"uncuttable"*

*All four "classical" elements (as they are now called) are present in a burning log.*

*Empedocles* came up with the very idea of elements. He said everything could be divided into four elements: earth, fire, water, and air. He wrote his theories down in a 5,000-line poem—even more clever!

Using a burning log as an example, he matched the elements like this: ash is **EARTH**, the liquid sap is **WATER**, smoke is **AIR**, and heat is **FIRE**.

# Air

## Aristotle and Quintessence

*Everything hot and wet was seen to be of the air element.*

*Another ancient Greek called Aristotle added a fifth element for space.*

*Democritus* was ahead of his time. Instead of believing that coins gradually disappeared as they wore away (as everyone else thought), he realized that everything must be made of *very small pieces*. He called the smallest an "atom." It was really a guess as he had no proof, but it was a very good guess.

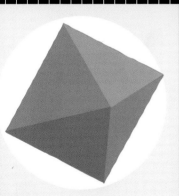

Eight-sided shapes
can also fit together and seemed the most airlike.

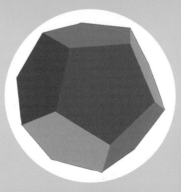

A twelve-sided shape
was chosen to represent a quintessence atom.

Democritus

*Worn-away coins have lost tiny, invisible particles.*

*in Greek.*

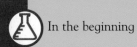
# The dark side

## DOCTOR DEATH

Among other things, alchemists experimented on medicines to cure diseases and prolong life. However, as doctors, they often did more harm than good. The First Emperor of China, having been led to believe he was an immortal god, must have gotten quite a shock when he experienced his first aches and pains. He turned to his *alchemist*, Xu Fu, to come up with an elixir for eternal life. Xu Fu prescribed mercury pills, a deadly poison. They made the First Emperor insane and eventually killed him.

很好吃!

(translation: *Yum, yum!*)

RIP
**The First Emperor**
*Not an immortal god after all!*

210 BCE                    270 CE

## THE LOST LIBRARY

Alchemy had its origins in the practices of ancient Egyptian priests, whose writings appeared in one of the greatest libraries of all time—at the Temple of the Muses in Alexandria. Alchemists from all around Egypt used the library, and so the Egyptian priests' knowledge was passed to the Greeks and Arabs. It would be fascinating to see what was in that vast library now, but, unfortunately, it was destroyed a long time ago.

*From men in white togas to magic*

The great Greek thinkers turned away from looking at the elements. "Know yourself" was their new mantra. The science of the elements now passed into a darker world—that of the *alchemists*.

# GOLD

## *The philosophers' stone*

Medieval European alchemists sought to turn metals, such as lead, into *gold*, using the Arabian theory (below). Many a day and night were spent in grubby, soot-blackened dens on the quest for the philosophers' stone—*a substance* the alchemists believed would help them make gold and grant them the secret of *eternal life*.

*Harry Potter tries to stop Voldemort from getting his hands on the stone in the first of J. K. Rowling's books,* Harry Potter and the Sorcerer's Stone.

776

## EARLY CHEMISTRY SETS

Sulfur

The Arabian alchemists introduced the importance of experimenting. They had vials and tubes, and mixed, heated, and boiled—all just to see what would happen. They had many successes in separating out chemicals and discovering new ones. They also said that metals were a combination of the four Greek elements, sulfur, and mercury. Could gold be made?

*and potions. Things had changed.*

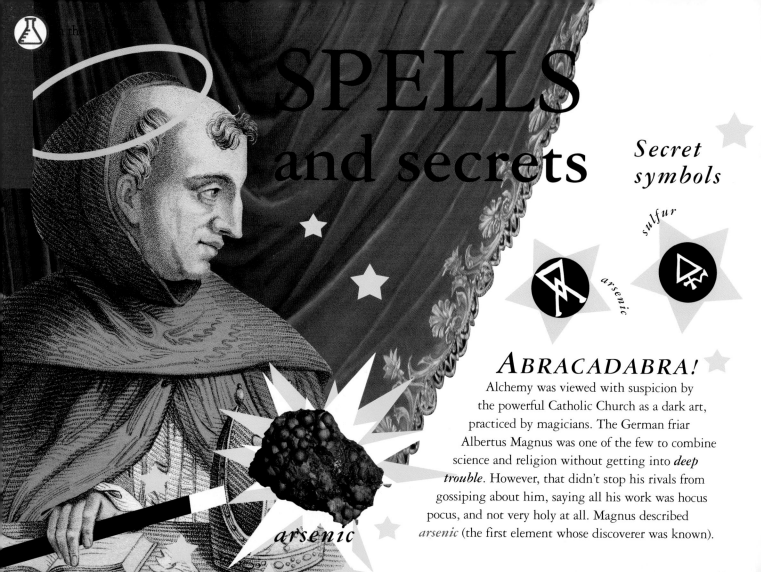

# SPELLS
## and secrets

*Secret symbols*

*sulfur*

*arsenic*

### ABRACADABRA!

Alchemy was viewed with suspicion by the powerful Catholic Church as a dark art, practiced by magicians. The German friar Albertus Magnus was one of the few to combine science and religion without getting into *deep trouble*. However, that didn't stop his rivals from gossiping about him, saying all his work was hocus pocus, and not very holy at all. Magnus described *arsenic* (the first element whose discoverer was known).

*arsenic*

## 1250            1382

*To keep their work secret, alchemists used strange drawings and symbols to represent the elements.*

*Harry Potter*

### GOLDEN BOY

Nicolas Flamel was a poor scholar from Paris. It has been claimed that he made the philosophers' stone and used it to make GOLD. After that, of course, he became a very *rich* scholar. He is mentioned in the story *Harry Potter and the Sorcerer's Stone* as the only alchemist to have made the stone. Who knows if the story is true? (But it probably isn't!)

14

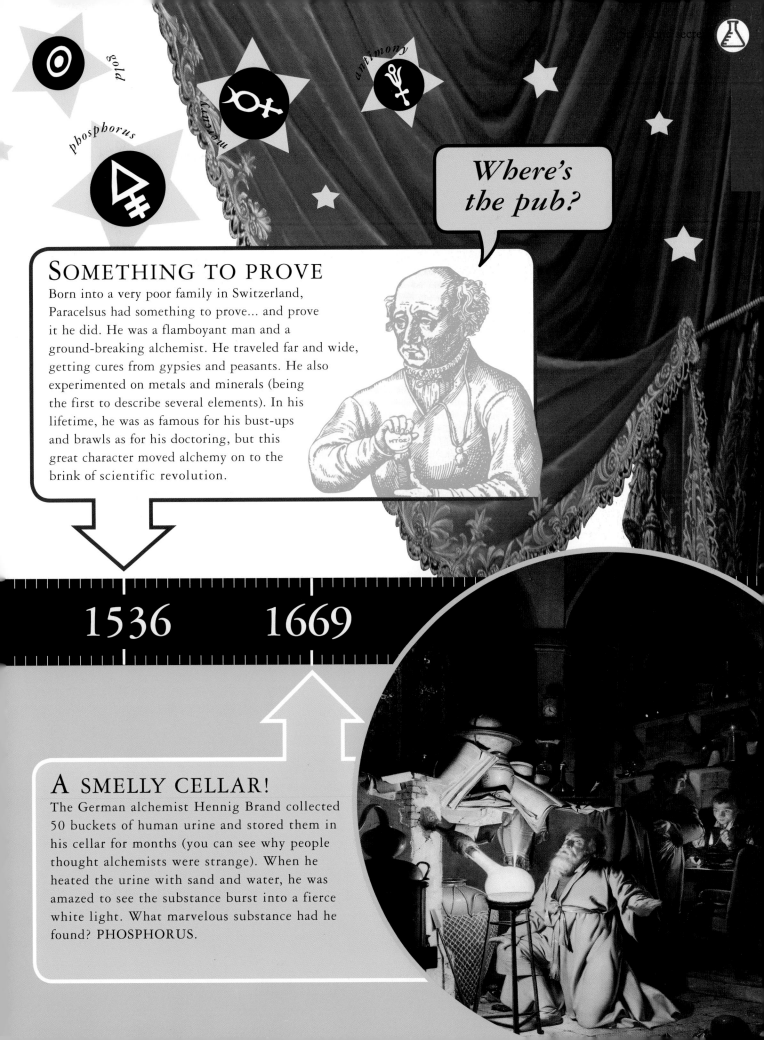

phosphorus

gold

mercury

antimony

## SOMETHING TO PROVE

Born into a very poor family in Switzerland, Paracelsus had something to prove... and prove it he did. He was a flamboyant man and a ground-breaking alchemist. He traveled far and wide, getting cures from gypsies and peasants. He also experimented on metals and minerals (being the first to describe several elements). In his lifetime, he was as famous for his bust-ups and brawls as for his doctoring, but this great character moved alchemy on to the brink of scientific revolution.

*Where's the pub?*

## 1536    1669

## A SMELLY CELLAR!

The German alchemist Hennig Brand collected 50 buckets of human urine and stored them in his cellar for months (you can see why people thought alchemists were strange). When he heated the urine with sand and water, he was amazed to see the substance burst into a fierce white light. What marvelous substance had he found? PHOSPHORUS.

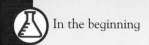

# *Airs* and graces

I'm a chemistry *bigwig!*

During the 16th century, science had advanced by leaps and bounds.

Copernicus had figured out our solar system, Newton had discovered gravity, and most importantly, scientists did proper EXPERIMENTS to prove that what they said was right (or that others were wrong!). Alchemists also now began *experimenting with "AIRS."*

## 1600's   1661

What *gas!*

## GAS ATTACK

As the Dutch alchemist Jan Helmont attempted to make "airs," his glass apparatus often broke. Feeling really annoyed, he used the word "chaos," but in his Dutch accent, it came out sounding like "gas."

## Don't call me Al

In 1661, Robert Boyle published *The Sceptical Chemist,* defining an element as a substance that could not be broken down into simpler substances.

People began to doubt the ancient Greeks' elements. Chemistry was emerging as a science in its own right. By dropping the "al" from alchemy, chemists tried to shake off the past.

*Joseph Priestley's device*

He offered his new carbonated drink to brave guests. It caught on. Rebranded as soda water, it became a health craze in Europe.

# Gases galore

In 1774, Joseph Priestley, an avid experimenter, discovered oxygen (though he called it "dephlogisticated air"—see below). Priestley went on to identify eight gases, disproving the previously held view that there was just one "air." Handling gases was a challenge, so Priestley introduced a device for collecting gases under water. One of the gases he managed to collect was carbon dioxide, which he used to make carbonated water.

## A BIT OF A MOUTHFUL

George Stahl, a German chemist, introduced this theory: when a substance was burned it released part of itself as a colorless, odorless, and weightless substance, called **PHLOGISTON** (say: flo-gist-on). Stahl said *phlogisticated* substances contained *phlogiston* but they became *dephlogisticated* when burned. **Get it? Good.**

*Antoine Lavoisier was guillotined during the French Revolution.*

# 1702 1774 1779

Although Boyle tried to make gold, he worked scientifically, writing his experiments in a clear, logical way. This was revolutionary!

# THE FATHER OF MODERN CHEMISTRY

The work of the wealthy French chemist Antoine Lavoisier was truly the start of chemistry as an *above-board* science. Here are just a few of his many achievements: he gave oxygen its name and realized it made fires burn, he discredited the widely believed but **WRONG** phlogiston theory, and finally put to bed the Greek elements—a theory that had *gone nowhere* for *thousands of years*. He named hydrogen, plus some other elements, and he wrote a fairly accurate **list of all the known elements** (33 so far, though some were wrong). What a genius! Sadly, he came to a violent end. As one of his fellow scientists commented at the time: "Only a minute to cut off that head, and a hundred years may not give us another like it."

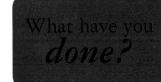
What have you *done?*

# It's *electrifying!*

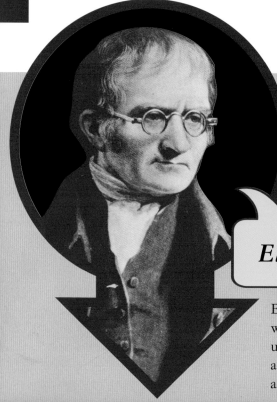

## WHAT IS AN *ATOM*?

> *Elementary*, my dear...

Englishman *John Dalton* came up with his revolutionary **atomic theory** using quirky homemade equipment—and despite being a clumsy experimenter and color-blind. *Here it is:*

> I'm a hydrogen atom!

1. Elements are made of tiny particles called ATOMS.

## 1803                    1807

> *It's **high** time we used electricity.*

If a *flammable gas* came near, the flame in the lamp *glowed brightly*, and miners knew to GET OUT.

## THE GENIUS OF THE LAMP

Sir Humphry Davy, aside from being an avid inhaler of laughing gas (a little habit of his), was the first to use *electricity* to isolate elements. His process is now called *electrolysis*. He used batteries (which were only invented in 1800) to perform his neat trick. Among other achievements, he is also famous for inventing the "safety lamp" for miners.

# From the 1800s, chemists had a **new toy**— *electricity!* This helped them isolate the elements by splitting substances.

**I'm very light.**

2. All **ATOMS** of an element are identical. Each element has a characteristic **ATOMIC WEIGHT**.

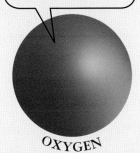

**I'm oxygen. I'm heavier than hydrogen...**

OXYGEN

3. THE ATOMS of an element are *different* from the atoms of any other element.

**... but we are great friends. Together we make the COMPOUND WATER.**

HYDROGEN  HYDROGEN

OXYGEN

4. ATOMS of one element can *combine* with atoms of other elements to form **COMPOUNDS**.

HEAT

5. *A chemical reaction,* such as heat, changes the way the atoms are grouped together.

# 1828

## GET THE LINGO

The Swedish chemist Jakob Berzelius was brilliant at *electrolysis.* He figured out the atomic weights of nearly ALL the elements known at that time. He also created a system of written *symbols* for the elements so we could write chemical formulas. Chemistry had its own language—at last!

$$O + H + H \rightarrow H_2O$$

oxygen  hydrogen  hydrogen  water

## Frankenstein

Mary Shelley's book *Frankenstein,* published in 1818, was inspired by the experiments and revelations of the chemists and the alchemists. In the story, Victor Frankenstein creates a man out of body parts that he sparks into life with a lightning bolt. His creation is a monster that drives Victor to his death.

*Frankenstein* marks the start of science fiction.

# *Organizing* the ELEMENTS

## Finding ORDER from *chaos* is the scientist's game. The elements needed to be brought into line and organized.

Calculating *atomic* weights:

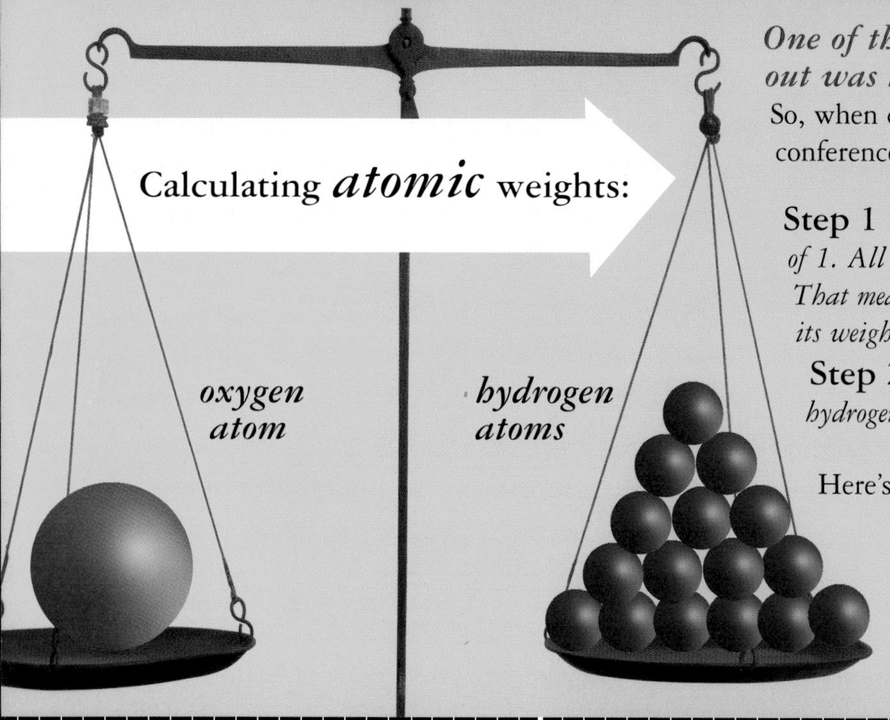

oxygen atom

hydrogen atoms

*One of the first things that needed sorting out was how to give atoms a weight.*

So, when chemists met at one of the first chemistry conferences in 1860, this is what they decided:

**Step 1** *Hydrogen, the lightest element, was given a weight of 1. All other elements' weights are compared to hydrogen. That means, if an element is 8 times heavier than hydrogen, its weight is 8.*

**Step 2** *Next multiply the weight (e.g., 8) by how many hydrogen atoms it can combine with.*

Here's how to find the atomic weight of oxygen:

$$8 \times 2 = 16$$

Oxygen is 8 times heavier than hydrogen and it combines with 2 hydrogen atoms (to make $H_2O$ or water). Therefore its atomic weight is 16.

# 1817          1862

*If you add the atomic weights of lithium and potassium, then divide that by two, you get the atomic weight for sodium.*

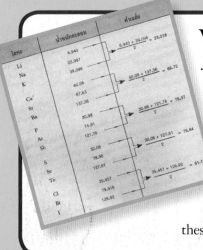

### WEIRD MATH
Johann Dobereiner recognized patterns in the elements. He found that when you clumped certain elements together in groups of three, strange math would result. This was surely more than a coincidence? He called these threesomes "triads."

*It's called the Telluric Screw. (Also not very catchy!)*

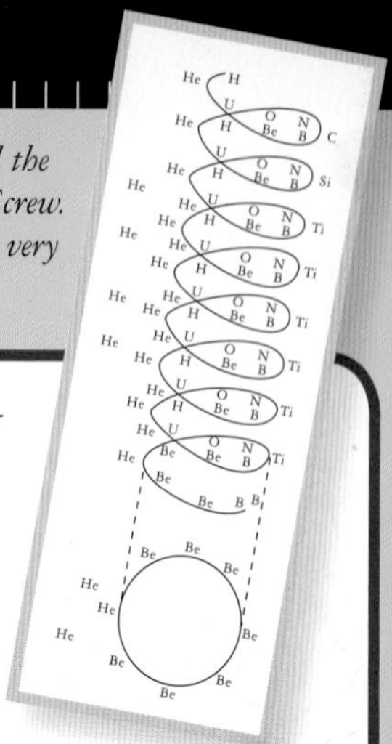

### CURLY WURLY
The "father of the periodic table" (see pages 26-27) is said to be Alexandre-Emile de Chancourtois. His curly-wurly diagram showed elements occuring at regular intervals (or "periodically," if you like). However, it was too difficult to read so it didn't really catch on.

# Predicting the future

If you look closely at this picture you can see where Mendeleev wrote question marks. Mendeleev KNEW there were missing elements needed to finish his chemical puzzle, and he predicted their weights and chemical properties. When some of those missing elements were found, his genius was realized. Mendeleev had classified *the building blocks of the universe.*

*One story goes that Mendeleev conceived the periodic table in a dream about a card game of patience.*

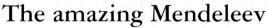

*The first draft of Mendeleev's table*

## The amazing Mendeleev
### (and his awesome mom)

In Siberia in 1834, *Dmitri Mendeleev* was born, the youngest of 14 children. His mother, realizing he was extremely brainy, walked and hitchhiked with him more than 1,000 miles (1,600 km) to St. Petersburg to enroll him in college there. Ten days after he was enrolled, she died. Her last words to her son were: "Insist on work and not on words. Patiently seek divine and scientific truth." Mendeleev took her words to heart and, at the age of 35, he arranged the 63 known elements into the first periodic table.

## 1864 1869

## Am I the WINNER?

## THE RACE IS ON!

Other chemists took up the baton. Julius Meyer made a table of the elements based on atomic weights and showed that the elements' physical properties repeated periodically. It's good, but he was beaten to the finish line.

## I had a DREAM...

# Pretty *powerful* stuff

## INVISIBLE RAYS

Wilhelm Roentgen wrapped some fluorescent minerals in thick black paper. He noticed a green light appearing unexpectedly a little way away from the parcel—invisible light rays from the mineral had somehow gone through the paper. He found that these light rays could also pass through human tissue, but leave the bones visible. He had invented **X-rays**.

*One of his first x-rays was this one of his wife's hand with a ring on her finger.*

 1895        1896

## *Oops-a-daisy, I discovered* RADIATION

Henri Becquerel also made an accidental discovery when investigating fluorescent minerals. He had placed a piece of fluorescent *uranium* on top of some photographic film wrapped in lightproof paper. When he returned, he discovered an image of the uranium sample on the film. How? Something invisible must have come off the uranium. Becquerel named the invisible rays *radiation*.

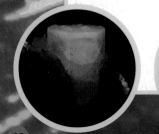  

*Fluorescent minerals*

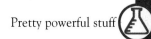

# Radiation was discovered by *accident*. From then on, it was only a matter of time (and the Curies) before more elements were found.

## TEAMWORK

Husband-and-wife team Pierre and Marie Curie were convinced there was a new radioactive element to be found in *pitchblende*. Pitchblende contains up to 30 different elements, so it was like looking for a needle in a haystack. It took four years' work, mostly in a scruffy, unheated, ill-equipped shed, to find not one, but *two* new elements: *polonium* (named after Marie's native Poland) and *radium* (named because it was so highly radioactive).

*Pitchblende*

*The Curies won the Nobel prize in 1903 for their work.*

1898

## DANGER!

After her husband's tragic death in a street accident, Marie Curie continued their work with radiation. Unaware of its dangers, Marie carried around tubes of radioactive material in her pocket. She liked the way they glowed with a "pretty blue-green light." She died in 1934, probably due to all this exposure to radiation, and was buried next to Pierre in Paris.

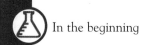 

# Going NUCLEAR

*Today, the atom*

**By the 1900s**, scientists had begun to look at what was *inside* atoms. It soon became clear that there were lots of *bits* and *pieces*.

- All **atoms** have parts with a **POSITIVE** electrical charge. These are called protons.

- All **atoms** have parts with a **NEGATIVE** charge. These are called electrons.

- Atoms are usually well balanced with the same number of negative electrons as positive protons.

But what does an **atom** look like?

*Electrons orbiting the nucleus*

## 1904          1911

### FRUITCAKE

J.J. Thomson thought that an atom looked a little like a teeny, weeny Christmas fruitcake. He thought the positive charge was an "atmosphere" through which the electrons moved.

### LITTLE WHIZZERS

Ernest Rutherford showed that atoms had a positively charged, very dense NUCLEUS with negatively charged ELECTRONS whizzing around it. This makes him the first ever "nuclear" scientist.

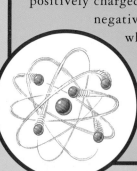

_is thought to look like this._

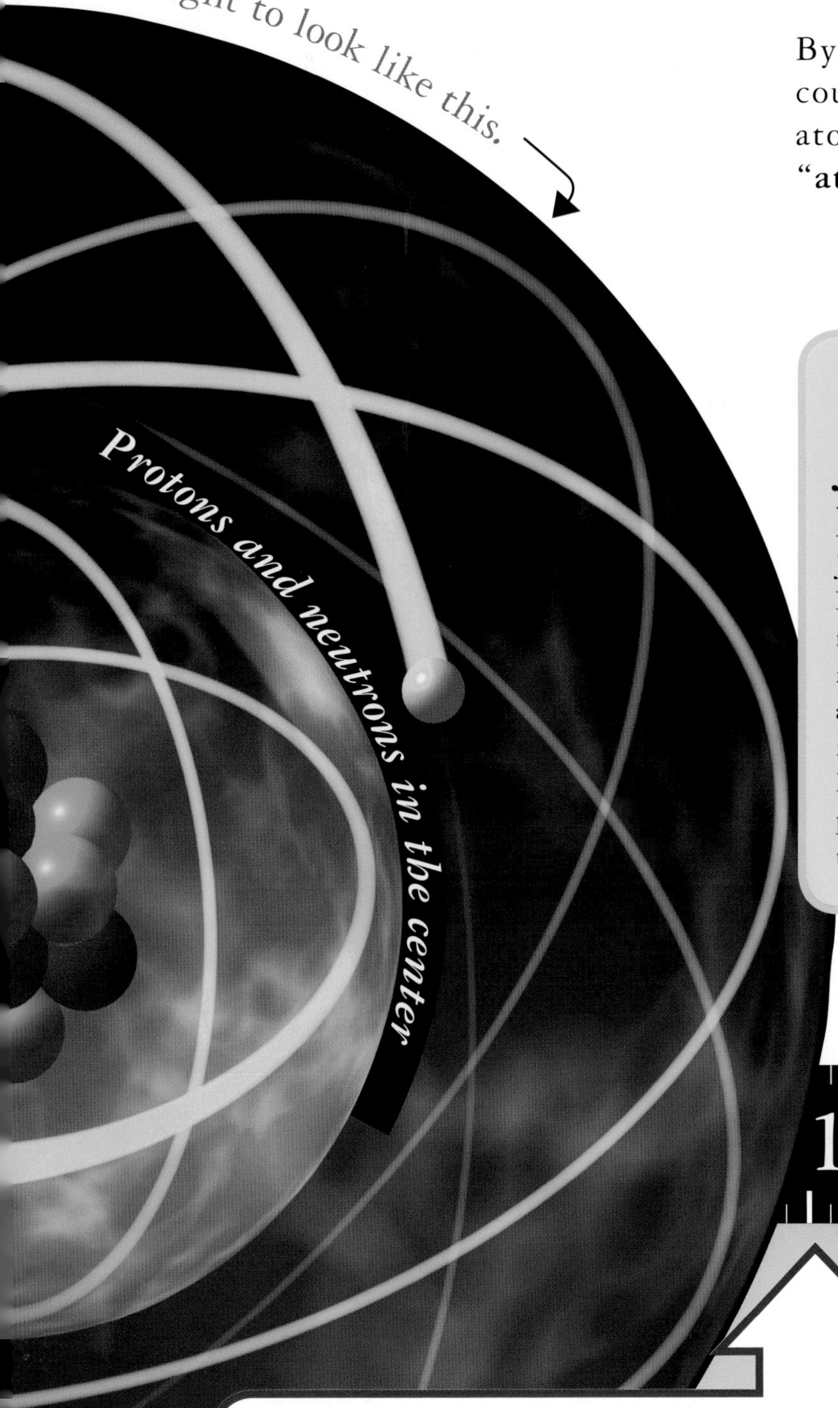

Protons and neutrons in the center

By this time, scientists were able to count the number of protons in an atom. This gave each element a unique "atomic number."

_Chadwick's toolbox_

## JIMMY NEUTRON

James Chadwick discovered NEUTRONS, and was given the nickname "Jimmy Neutron" by some as a result. A neutron is the **uncharged** part of an atom's **nucleus**. His discovery led to the invention of the atomic bomb. He said, "When I realized that a nuclear bomb was not only possible, it was inevitable, I had then to start taking sleeping pills. It was the only remedy."

# 1913 1932 1940

## MINI PLANETS

Niels Bohr described an atom as though it were a minute solar system with tiny electrons orbiting the nucleus, like planets. He said electrons in an atom's outer orbit are shared with or given away to other atoms. This made atoms bond together, forming molecules.

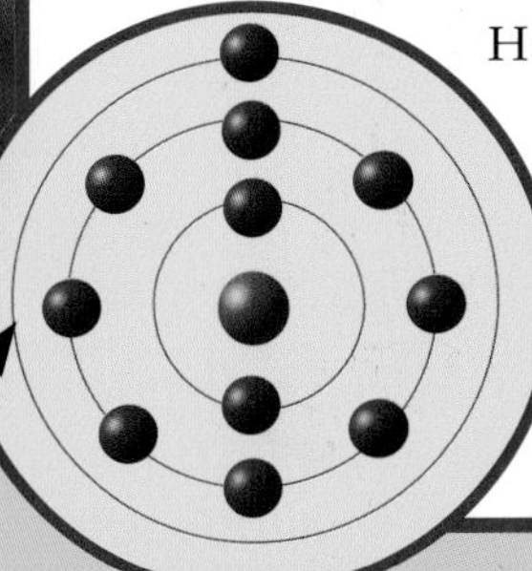

_Outer orbit of a sodium atom_

## GETTING CREATIVE

Glenn Seaborg was an American atomic scientist who co-created 10 NEW ELEMENTS in a nuclear reactor. He influenced so many of their names that he could write his address in elements: Seaborgium, Lawrencium (_for the Lawrence Berkeley Laboratory where he worked_), Berkelium, Californium, Americium.

# The PERIODIC table

SO HERE IT IS. Today's periodic table is the result of many *brilliant people*'s lifetime work—if elements could talk, they could each tell their own unique story of discovery. The table not only represents the history of chemistry, but also the component parts of the entire universe—*all on one double page.*

A horizontal row is called a PERIOD.

Each vertical column is called a GROUP, or family, of elements. Some groups have elements sharing very similar *properties*, such as their appearances and their behavior. Other groups have elements with less in common.

10,292°F (5,700°C) TUNGSTEN boils, becoming a gas.

1,947°F (1,064°C) GOLD melts from a solid to a liquid.

-38°F (-39°C) MERCURY melts, becoming a liquid.

-452°F (-269°C) HELIUM boils from a liquid to a gas.

**Temperature**
Each element has its own melting and boiling points when it changes from a solid to a liquid to a gas.

**1**

 H HYDROGEN 1

Li LITHIUM 3

Na SODIUM 11

K POTASSIUM 19

Rb RUBIDIUM 37

Cs CESIUM 55

Fr FRANCIUM 87

**2**

Be BERYLLIUM 4

Mg MAGNESIUM 12

Ca CALCIUM 20

Sr STRONTIUM 38

 Ba 56 BARIUM

Ra RADIUM 88

**3** Sc SCANDIUM 21

Y YTTRIUM 39

LANTHANIDES or RARE-EARTH METALS 57 – 71

ACTINIDES or RARE-EARTH RADIOACTIVE METALS 89 – 103

**4** Ti TITANIUM 22

Zr ZIRCONIUM 40

Hf HAFNIUM 72

Rf RUTHERFORDIUM 104

**5** V VANADIUM 23

Nb NIOBIUM 41

Ta TANTALUM 73

Db DUBNIUM 105

**6**  Cr CHROMIUM 24

Mo MOLYBDENUM 42

 W TUNGSTEN 74

Sg SEABORGIUM 106

**7** Mn MANGANESE 25

Tc TECHNETIUM 43

Re RHENIUM 75

Bh BOHRIUM 107

**8** FE IRON 26

Ru RUTHENIUM 44

Os OSMIUM 76

Hs HASSIUM 108

**9** Co COBALT 27

Rh RHODIUM 45

Ir IRIDIUM 77

Mt MEITNERIUM 109

La LANTHANUM 57

Ce CERIUM 58

Pr PRASEODYMIUM 59

Nd NEODYMIUM 60

 Pm PROMETHIUM 61

Sm SAMARIUM 62

Ac ACTINIUM 89

Th THORIUM 90

Pa PROTACTINIUM 91

U URANIUM 92

Np NEPTUNIUM 93

Pu PLUTONIUM 94

As scientists found the heavier elements and began to create many more, Glenn Seaborg suggested placing the lanthanides and actinides below the table.

**KEY:**

*Alkali metals:* These silvery metals are very reactive.

*Alkaline earth metals:* These shiny, silvery-white metals are reactive.

*Transition metals:* Many are strong and have high boiling and melting points.

*"Reactive"* means an element is quick to join up with other elements.

*Lanthanides:* Many are soft and shiny, silvery-white metals.

*Actinides:* These are radioactive heavy elements.

*Poor metals:* Softer, weaker metals.

*Nonmetals:* Most are gases at room temperature and easily snap as solids.

*Halogens:* These nonmetals are highly reactive and harmful.

*Noble gases:* These nonmetals are the least reactive of all the elements.

**Kr**
KRYPTON
36

Atomic symbol
Atom's name
Atomic number

The "atomic number" is the number of protons in each atom of an element. The higher the atomic number, the "heavier" an element is said to be.

**18**

**He**
HELIUM
2

FLUORINE (F) in toothpaste helps to strengthen tooth enamel.

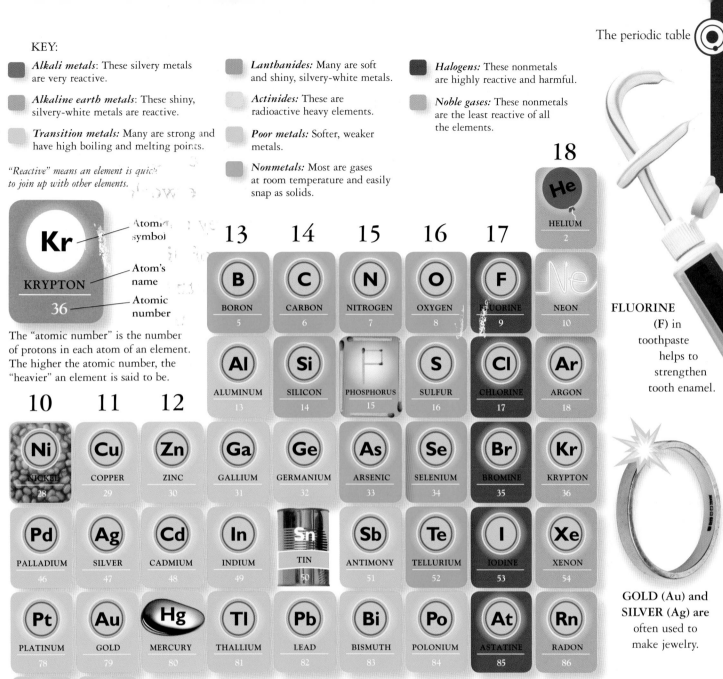

**13**

**B** BORON 5
**Al** ALUMINUM 13

**14**

**C** CARBON 6
**Si** SILICON 14

**15**

**N** NITROGEN 7
**P** PHOSPHORUS 15

**16**

**O** OXYGEN 8
**S** SULFUR 16

**17**

**F** FLUORINE 9
**Cl** CHLORINE 17

**Ne** NEON 10
**Ar** ARGON 18

**10**
**11**
**12**

**Ni** NICKEL 28
**Cu** COPPER 29
**Zn** ZINC 30
**Ga** GALLIUM 31
**Ge** GERMANIUM 32
**As** ARSENIC 33
**Se** SELENIUM 34
**Br** BROMINE 35
**Kr** KRYPTON 36

**Pd** PALLADIUM 46
**Ag** SILVER 47
**Cd** CADMIUM 48
**In** INDIUM 49
**Sn** TIN 50
**Sb** ANTIMONY 51
**Te** TELLURIUM 52
**I** IODINE 53
**Xe** XENON 54

**Pt** PLATINUM 78
**Au** GOLD 79
**Hg** MERCURY 80
**Tl** THALLIUM 81
**Pb** LEAD 82
**Bi** BISMUTH 83
**Po** POLONIUM 84
**At** ASTATINE 85
**Rn** RADON 86

**Ds** DARMSTADTIUM 110
**Rg** ROENTGENIUM 111

GOLD (Au) and SILVER (Ag) are often used to make jewelry.

Scientists can predict how an element will react based on where it is on the table.

Einstein

**Eu** EUROPIUM 63
**Gd** GADOLINIUM 64
**Tb** TERBIUM 65
**Dy** DYSPROSIUM 66
**Ho** HOLMIUM 67
**Er** ERBIUM 68
**Tm** THULIUM 69
**Yb** YTTERBIUM 70
**Lu** LUTETIUM 71

**Am** AMERICIUM 95
**Cm** CURIUM 96
**Bk** BERKELIUM 97
**Cf** CALIFORNIUM 98
**Es** EINSTEINIUM 99
**Fm** FERMIUM 100
**Md** MENDELEVIUM 101
**No** NOBELIUM 102
**Lr** LAWRENCIUM 103

Some elements have been named after famous scientists.

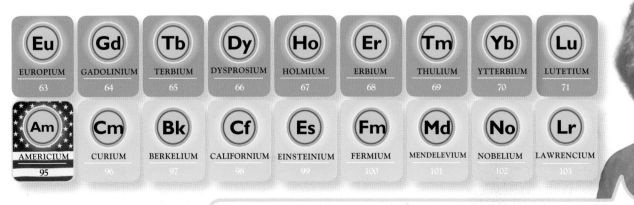

# We are STARDUST

"

*You're a star!*
*No, really, you* **are** *stardust ...*

... at least you once were.
All elements come from space,
and since we are made out of
elements it follows that:
a) we are from space
b) we are stars.

And we're not the only ones.
So are dogs, cats, bridges,
mountains, and, in fact, plants,
water, air, and...
*everything*
is from space.

"

*I'm a space dog.*

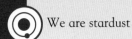

# Creating the

## IT ALL STARTED OVER 13 BILLION YEARS AGO

### when the universe began with what's been called *THE BIG BANG!*

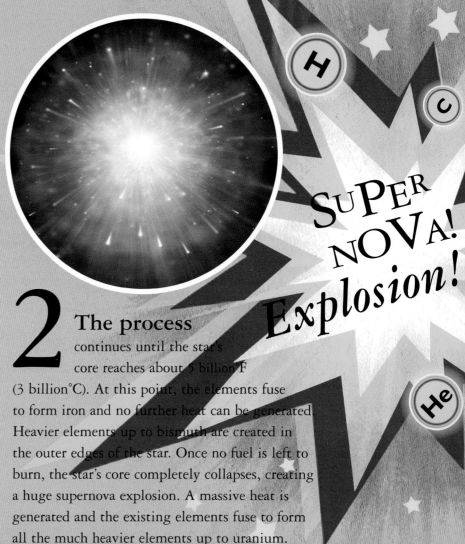

**SUPER NOVA! Explosion!**

## 1 A star is born

in a gigantic cluster of hydrogen atoms. It is powered by burning hydrogen, which fuses to form a helium core at 180 million°F (10 million°C). Once most of the hydrogen has burned, the star starts to cool. Its core collapses, which generates a vast heat. The star expands and at 180 million°F (100 million°C), the helium atoms fuse together, producing carbon, oxygen, and neon atoms. This process then repeats itself with these elements fusing together to form new ones as the star gets hotter and hotter.

## 2 The process

continues until the star's core reaches about 5 billion°F (3 billion°C). At this point, the elements fuse to form iron and no further heat can be generated. Heavier elements up to bismuth are created in the outer edges of the star. Once no fuel is left to burn, the star's core completely collapses, creating a huge supernova explosion. A massive heat is generated and the existing elements fuse to form all the much heavier elements up to uranium.

## ABUNDANCE OF ELEMENTS: estimated percentages of atoms

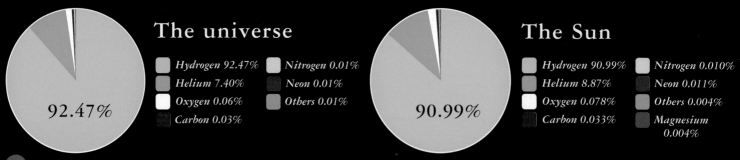

### The universe

92.47%

- Hydrogen 92.47%
- Helium 7.40%
- Oxygen 0.06%
- Carbon 0.03%
- Nitrogen 0.01%
- Neon 0.01%
- Others 0.01%

### The Sun

90.99%

- Hydrogen 90.99%
- Helium 8.87%
- Oxygen 0.078%
- Carbon 0.033%
- Nitrogen 0.010%
- Neon 0.011%
- Others 0.004%
- Magnesium 0.004%

# ELEMENTS

Hydrogen, helium, deuterium, and lithium were the first elements to exist. The rest of the *natural elements* were created *inside STARS*.

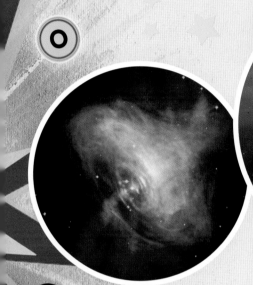

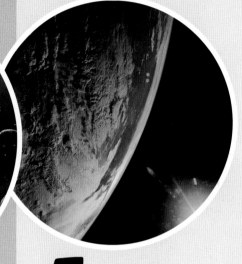

## 3 Stardust

This massive explosion marking the end of a star's life scatters all the elements throughout the universe. Elements are scattered as stardust and swirling debris, such as meteorites. The hydrogen atoms cluster together again to start forming a new star.

## 4 Birth of our solar nebula

Five billion years ago, within a cloud of stardust from one of these supernova explosions, our Sun was born and the swirling debris of elements collided to form the planets in our solar system.

## 5 Just four elements—

hydrogen, carbon, nitrogen, and oxygen—make up more than 95% by weight of all living things on Earth. They are also four out of the six most abundant elements in the universe. If these four elements are so abundant then possibly life could exist elsewhere even as microscopic simple organisms.

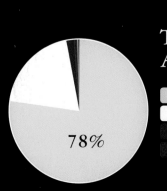

## The Earth's Atmosphere

78%

- Nitrogen 78%
- Oxygen 21%
- Argon 0.93%
- Carbon 0.03%
- Neon 0.0018%
- Helium 0.00052%

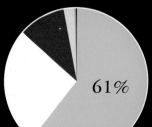

## A Human

61%

- Hydrogen 61%
- Oxygen 26%
- Carbon 10.5%
- Nitrogen 2.4%
- Calcium 0.23%
- Sulfur 0.13%
- Phosphorus 0.13%

# Hydrogen

The number one element!

The first element to EXIST.

A star is fueled by burning HYDROGEN.

*Hydrogen is the lightest element—even lighter than air.* Unless it's joined with other elements on Earth, hydrogen floats away and escapes into space.

**Water, water everywhere!**
Hydrogen is named from the Greek words *hydor* and *genes*, meaning "water forming.". On Earth, hydrogen is mainly found joined with oxygen as WATER.

# Hydrogen *is* 88% of all atoms in the

# Hydrogen is a highly flammable, colorless, odorless gas.

It's mostly produced from methane, which is the gas piped to our homes.

## Burning liquid hydrogen mixed with liquid oxygen propels rockets into space.

Hydrogen gas could be the clean, nonpolluting fuel of the future. Some cars and buses are already powered by hydrogen. Hydrogen gas, generated from water, is burned in oxygen from the air, and therefore turns back into water. (Remember water is $H_2O$.) There are no nasty exhaust fumes from these cars as the only waste product is water. Excellent!

*universe,* and the biggest ingredient of *the* STARS.

# HeLIUM

Helium is the **only** element to be discovered in space, **before it was found on Earth**. It is the second most abundant element in the universe and the **second lightest** element after hydrogen.

## DISCOVERY

In 1868, during a total eclipse of the Sun, the astronomer Pierre Janssen noticed a yellowish spectral line, or pattern of light, coming from the Sun. It was identified as a new element.

# HELIUM comes from the *Greek*

*Helium gas makes party balloons float.*

## Rocket control

Liquid helium is colorless and *very, very* cold. It is used in space rockets to keep the rocket fuel stable until the moment it is burned.

*Up to 7% of natural gas is helium.*

## Coolant

Liquid helium is also used to cool scientific electrical equipment, such as body scanners and huge computers.

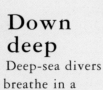

## Down deep

Deep-sea divers breathe in a mixture of helium and oxygen as an artificial atmosphere inside their submersibles.

*Helium gas doesn't smell.*

## Up high

Because it is so light, helium is ideal for lifting things, such as scientific weather balloons, airships, or even party balloons. About 10% of extracted helium is used for lifting things.

WORD *helios,* meaning SUN.

*Oxygen combines with itself 15 miles (24 km) above the Earth's surface to form the ozone layer.*

15 miles
(24 km)

*Ozone protects life by deflecting some harmful ultraviolet light from the Sun.*

# XYGEN

... equals life. It's invisible, it doesn't smell, and you can't tell it's there, but without it there would be *NO LIFE ON EARTH*.

**Oxygen** is the third most *abundant* element in the *universe.*

## In the beginning

About 3.8 billion years ago, tiny simple molecules of life appeared on the surface of the Earth. They used the Sun as an energy source to make their food, just like plants do today. The waste gas of this process was oxygen. Millions of years later, oxygen levels rose high enough to change the atmosphere to the one we enjoy today. The Earth could now sustain more complex life. Plants released oxygen into the air, which animals on land and in rivers, lakes, and oceans could breathe in.

At sea level, **oxygen** *is 21% of air.*

## Many machines

require oxygen to make them go.
When a fuel is burned in oxygen,
this process is called combustion.
A car has an internal combustion
engine, which heats the right amount
of fuel with the right amount of
oxygen. A modern jet engine gulps
in four squash courts of air per
second to get enough oxygen
to burn with the fuel.

*During plane flights,
the oxygen levels are
monitored and cabin
pressure is adjusted plus
emergency oxygen supplies
are stored onboard.*

# If oxygen
## levels go above
## 25%, we can't
### *survive.*

## If oxygen
## levels
fall below
17%, we can't
*survive.*

## Oxygen makes
up more than half
the weight of the
**average person**.

The amount of oxygen in
air becomes less when at high
altitude or under water.
Mountain climbers have
to adjust slowly to
the changing oxygen levels as they climb higher.
Divers carry their oxygen supplies with them and
astronauts also take oxygen when they travel into space.

# NITROGEN

## IS 78% OF THE AIR AROUND US.

We breathe in this invisible, odorless gas all the time, but it's of no use to us in this form. Yet we, and, in fact, all living things, use nitrogen to make proteins—the building blocks of our bodies' cells. So how do we get it? The answer is in the **NITROGEN CYCLE**.

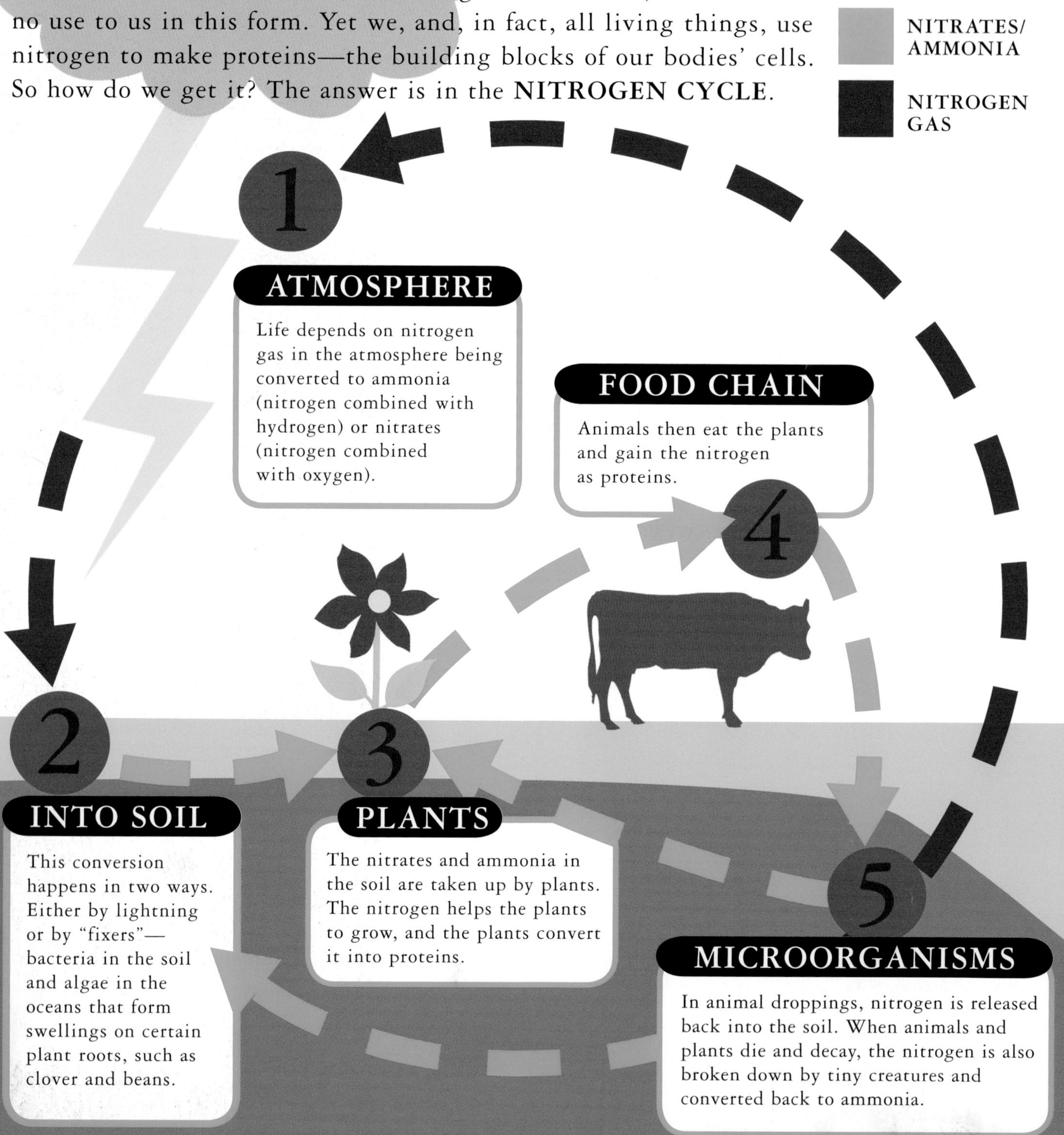

 **NITRATES/ AMMONIA**

 **NITROGEN GAS**

### 1 ATMOSPHERE

Life depends on nitrogen gas in the atmosphere being converted to ammonia (nitrogen combined with hydrogen) or nitrates (nitrogen combined with oxygen).

### FOOD CHAIN

Animals then eat the plants and gain the nitrogen as proteins.

4

### 2 INTO SOIL

This conversion happens in two ways. Either by lightning or by "fixers"— bacteria in the soil and algae in the oceans that form swellings on certain plant roots, such as clover and beans.

### 3 PLANTS

The nitrates and ammonia in the soil are taken up by plants. The nitrogen helps the plants to grow, and the plants convert it into proteins.

### 5 MICROORGANISMS

In animal droppings, nitrogen is released back into the soil. When animals and plants die and decay, the nitrogen is also broken down by tiny creatures and converted back to ammonia.

**NAMED FROM GREEK** *nitron* and *genes,* meaning "niter forming." **NITER** was the old name for *potassium nitrate*, known as saltpeter and used in gunpowder.

# Explosive!

Compounds of nitrogen can suddenly release a lot of energy because the nitrogen atoms are eager to revert violently to nitrogen gas. This causes a large amount of heat, which causes clouds of released gas to expand even more violently.

> This could blow up on me!

In 1867, the Swedish chemist *Alfred Nobel* invented dynamite, which was a safe way to handle the explosive nitrogen compound, nitroglycerine. With his riches, he set up and funded the annual Nobel Prizes, which are six awards for great achievement.

> I'm the Nobel of the Nobel Prizes.

Nitrogen is still a key element of weapons today. But this explosive behavior can be used more constructively in making safety airbags inflate.

## Fertilizers

Farmers want to increase the quantity of the crops they grow, and so they use ammonium nitrate (nitrogen combined with hydrogen and oxygen) to fertilize their fields. However, if fertilizers are overused, this can cause an imbalance in the Earth's cycles.

> Steady there. Don't overdo it!

## Freezes

Nitrogen becomes a liquid at a very low temperature. Since liquid nitrogen is so cold, it turns most things into solids and prevents any chemical processes from taking place. This is why it is used to freeze blood and preserve genetic material.

## Preserves

Nitrogen is generally an unreactive gas and bonds strongly with its own atoms. It can be used to make an oxygen-free atmosphere. Apples quickly become moldy in air that contains oxygen, but they keep really well for up to two years in containers filled with nitrogen gas.

## Synthetics

It's likely that what you are wearing and what you are sitting or lying on are made from chemicals. These chemicals, such as the plastic polyurethane, nylon fibers, and brilliantly colored dyes, started out as nitrogen gas.

# CARBON

is a friendly atom since it joins with itself, as in *sparkling diamonds* and *lumps of coal*, as well as with many other elements, forming over ten million compounds.

The carbon atoms join together in a rigid 3-D structure in a diamond.

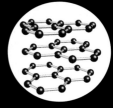

The carbon atoms join together in a different way in graphite, making it much weaker.

## HARDEST *to* SOFTEST

diamond    coke    charcoal    carbon black    graphite

### "Ice"
Unscratchable, icy cold, and rigid, diamonds are the hardest natural substance on Earth. Only 20% of mined diamonds become jewelry.

### Fuel
Coke is the hard, grey, porous remains of heated coal. It is ideal for fuelling the blast furnaces used in making iron and steel.

### Filter
Charcoal is the fine, black substance remaining after partly burning wood or bone. It's used as a filter for refining sugar and purifying water and air.

### Filler
Carbon black is the fine powder from burning natural gas. It's in the ink used for printing and it's added to rubber for strong tires.

### "Lead"
Flaky and slippery, graphite is one of the softest natural substances on Earth. It's in the lead of a pencil and the grease for a squeaky lock.

Could you reduce your CARBON FOOTPRINT?

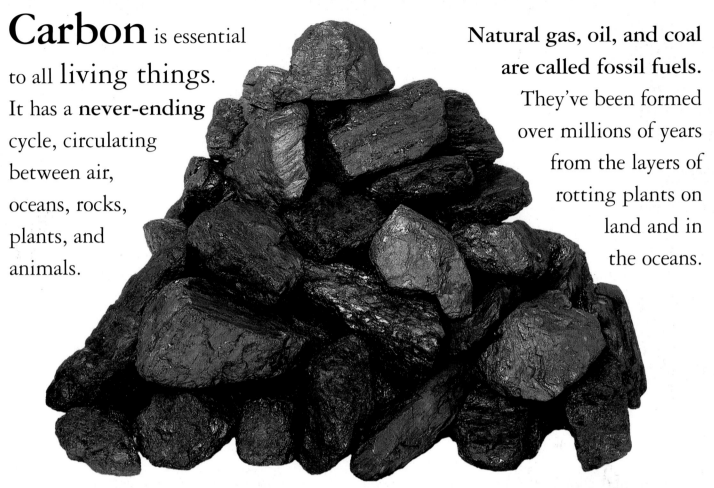

# Carbon is essential to all living things.

It has a **never-ending** cycle, circulating between air, oceans, rocks, plants, and animals.

Natural gas, oil, and coal are called fossil fuels. They've been formed over millions of years from the layers of rotting plants on land and in the oceans.

## 250 MILLION YEARS from *plants* to COAL

Under intense pressure, plants become fossilized as coal.

## Carbon cycle

Most of what we eat are carbon compounds, which give us energy. Any unused carbon is breathed out as carbon dioxide. Plants extract this carbon dioxide from the air to make their food and then the carbon is passed along the food chain.

## Carbon dating

The age of ancient relics made from wood, flesh, or bone can be worked out by analyzing the amount of radioactive carbon contained in the object.

## Carbon life

Carbon is essential to life as the structural basis for compounds in living cells, most importantly for DNA, the genetic code. Our bodies contain 35 lbs (16 kg) of carbon in various forms.

**CARBON DIOXIDE** (carbon and oxygen)
is formed when fossil fuels are burned, when trees are burned, and when fuel is burned in engines. "Carbon footprint" is a measure of carbon dioxide produced through our energy use and travel.

# So WHAT'S a DOG made from?

Just imagine you could build a living dog! For the ingredients, you'll need a quarter of all *natural elements*. These are the same elements that are in **YOU!**

## Carbon

**18.5%**

Carbon is essential as the building block of all life.

## 1% Phosphorus

A small amount of phosphorus is found in the dog's DNA and makes its teeth and bones strong.

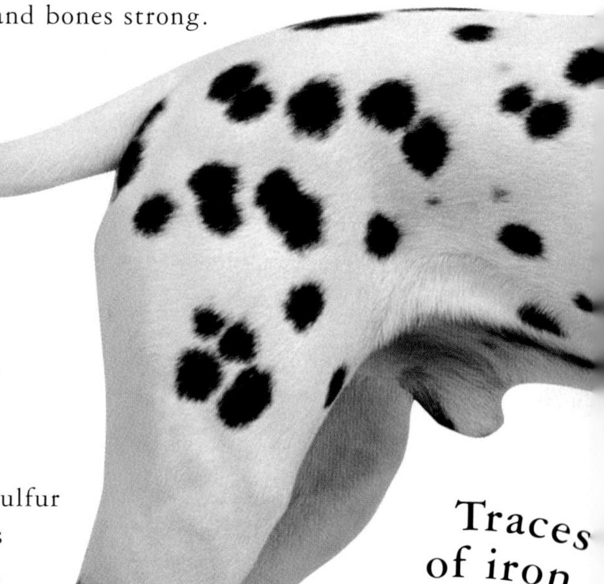

## Magnesium

A small amount of magnesium makes the dog's bones strong.

## Sulfur

A small amount of sulfur is found in the dog's hair, nails, and skin.

## Calcium

**1.5%**

Calcium helps to make the dog's bones strong.

## Traces of iron

Iron transports oxygen around in the dog's red blood cells.

# So Want to make an elephant?

# and *throw* in...

**Oxygen 65%**

*Potassium*

A small amount of potassium is required for muscles, nerve reflexes, and impulses.

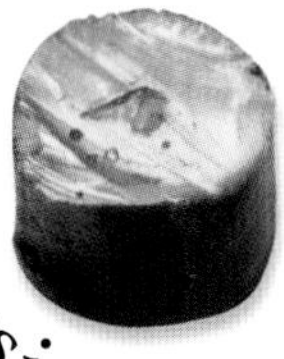

The dog needs iodine for two essential hormones.

**Traces of iodine**

Loads of oxygen is vital, especially for the dog's brain to work.

**Traces of manganese**

$H_2O$

**Hydrogen**

**9.5%**

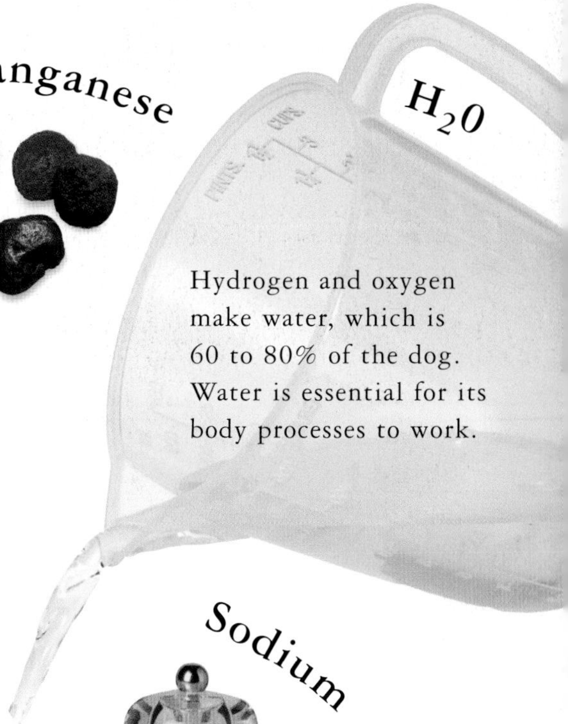

Hydrogen and oxygen make water, which is 60 to 80% of the dog. Water is essential for its body processes to work.

Hydrogen connects the chains of the dog's DNA.

**Sodium**

**Nitrogen**

**3.3%**

**Traces of chlorine**

**Traces of fluorine**

Sodium and chlorine form salt. The dog needs small amounts for a healthy heart.

Nitrogen is in the dog's DNA and is essential for forming all its cells.

***Add*** a sprinkling of other ***elements*** for good health.

# You'll need a bigger bowl!

# What's *in*

Two atoms of **HYDROGEN** and one atom of **OXYGEN** make a molecule of water. But they are not the only elements in the water we drink.

## TASTY WATER

When water falls as rain, this is the freshwater we can drink. But, as the rain soaks into the ground, it picks up the elements of the rocks. Depending on the types of rocks, drinking water will taste different in different areas.

Carbon dioxide creates the FIZZ when opening sparkling water.

**CALCIUM**

**MAGNESIUM**

**CARBON**

**SILICON**

**SULFUR**

Rainwater picks up elements on its travels.

### Dissolved elements

Around the world, drinking water is taken from wells, reservoirs, bore holes, or springs from underground water sources. Elements in the local rocks have dissolved into this water supply.

97.2% of all WATER on Earth is undrinkable!

# YOUR WATER?

## BOTTLED WATER!

When you drink from a bottle of water, check out the label. You can't see the elements, but they are in there!

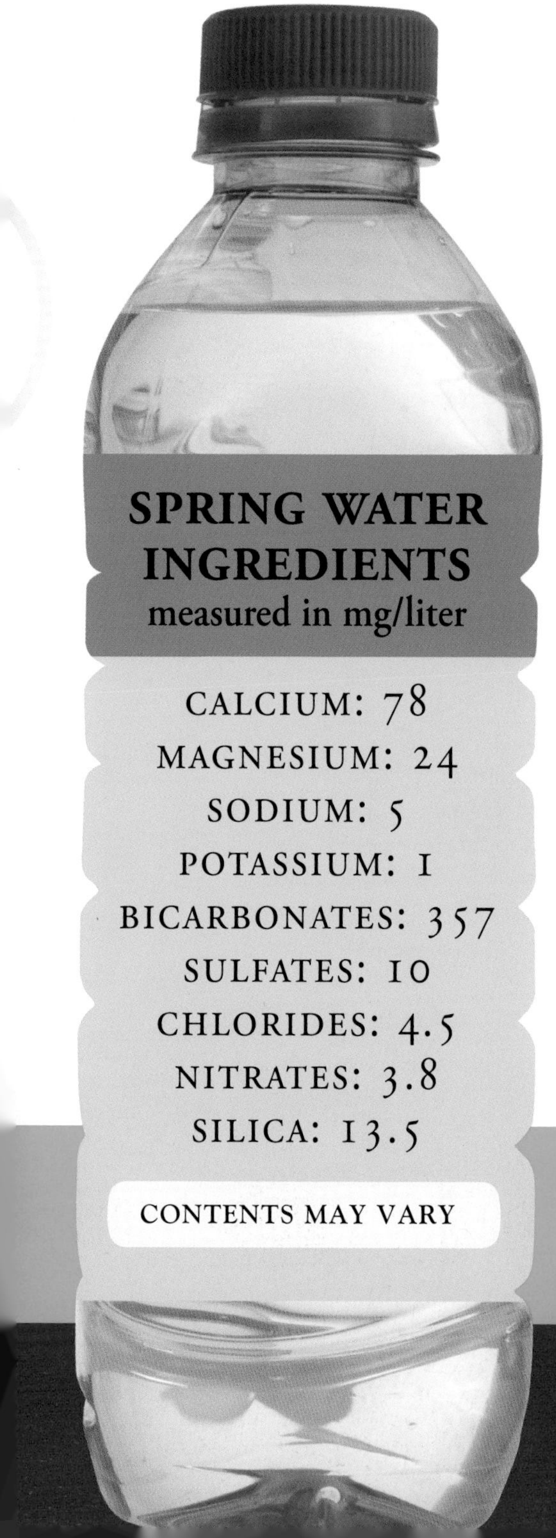

### SPRING WATER INGREDIENTS
measured in mg/liter

CALCIUM: 78

MAGNESIUM: 24

SODIUM: 5

POTASSIUM: 1

BICARBONATES: 357

SULFATES: 10

CHLORIDES: 4.5

NITRATES: 3.8

SILICA: 13.5

CONTENTS MAY VARY

## TAP WATER

When we turn on a faucet, the water that pours out has been on a journey. Taken from underground sources or reservoirs, the water has been purified to remove dirt and germs and then disinfected. Many elements are still present, including:

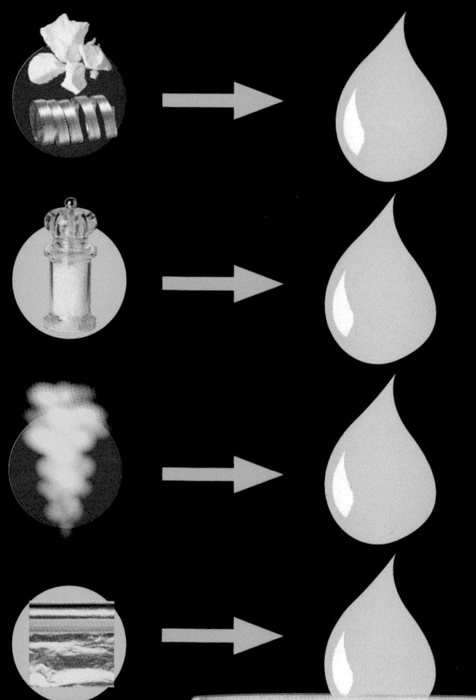

### Calcium and magnesium
Large quantities of these elements make "hard" water.

### Sodium
This element is found in soft water.

### Fluorine
This prevents tooth decay, but too much can be unhealthy.

### Aluminum
This traps harmful solids in the purifying process.

### Iron
Unpleasant red-brown water has undissolved iron.

### Sulfur
Harmless sulfur-eating bacteria can make water smelly.

# *Take a pinch of zinc... add an element of*

Oily fish

**Iodine** is needed
in very small amounts.
It is found in seafood,
dairy products,
and in table salt.

# Eat up *your*

You probably know
that what you **eat** contains
**proteins**, **carbohydrates**,
**fats**, and **fibers,** but did you
know these are compounds of carbon,
hydrogen, oxygen, and nitrogen?
There are also many other
elements in our food to keep
our bodies working properly.

Every *meal* we eat contains *traces* of different *elements*.

A trace

**Iodine**  Black crystals

10 mg/day

**Phosphorus**
is essential every day.
Bread is a good source.

Wholewheat bread

**Zinc**
Gray-blue
metal

**Zinc** is found in
sunflower seeds, whole-
wheat bread, seafood,
beef, and lamb.

Sunflower seeds

Broccoli

**Magnesium**  Silvery-white metal

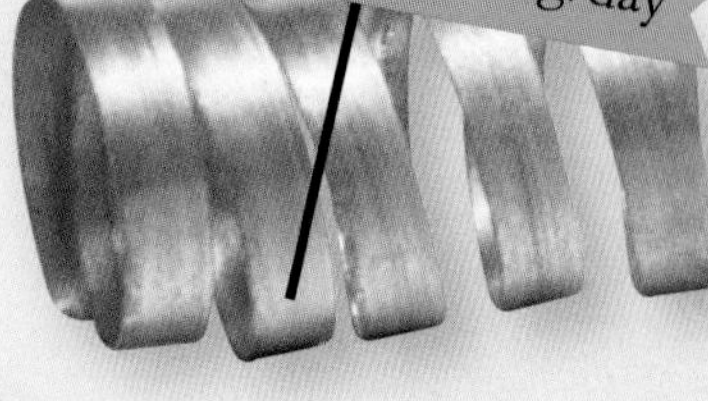

400 mg/day

**Magnesium** is found
in dairy products, seeds, dried
fruits, and vegetables.

Dried apricots

# elements!

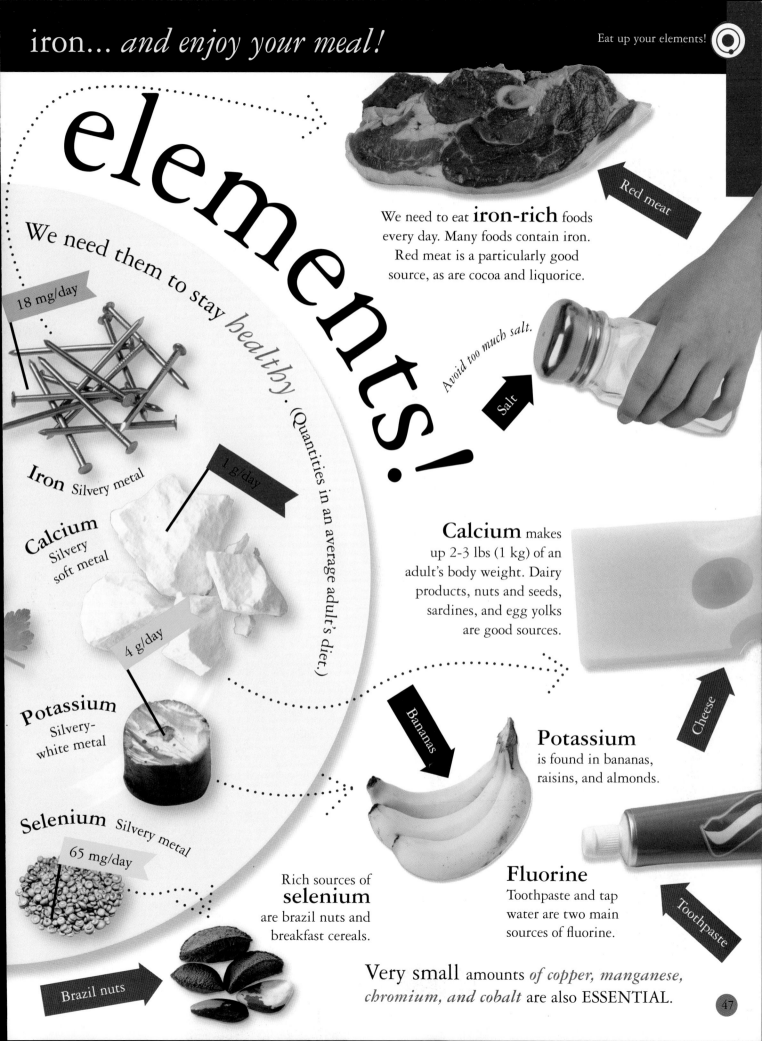

**Red meat**

We need to eat **iron-rich** foods every day. Many foods contain iron. Red meat is a particularly good source, as are cocoa and liquorice.

We need them to stay *healthy*. (Quantities in an average adult's diet.)

*Avoid too much salt.*

**Salt**

**18 mg/day**

**Iron** Silvery metal

**1 g/day**

**Calcium**
Silvery
soft metal

**4 g/day**

**Calcium** makes up 2-3 lbs (1 kg) of an adult's body weight. Dairy products, nuts and seeds, sardines, and egg yolks are good sources.

**Cheese**

**Potassium**
Silvery-
white metal

**Bananas**

**Potassium**
is found in bananas, raisins, and almonds.

**Selenium** Silvery metal

**65 mg/day**

Rich sources of **selenium** are brazil nuts and breakfast cereals.

**Fluorine**
Toothpaste and tap water are two main sources of fluorine.

**Toothpaste**

**Brazil nuts**

**Very small** amounts *of copper, manganese, chromium, and cobalt* are also ESSENTIAL.

# Sodium

This highly reactive metal is silvery-white and so soft that it can easily be cut with a knife. Sodium is more commonly found in compounds forming **salts**.

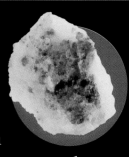

*Roman soldiers traded with salt.*

Since ancient times, access to salt supplies meant riches and power. The salt was used to preserve food, allowing armies and traders to travel over long distances. The word "salary" comes from the *salarium* paid to Roman soldiers to buy the salt they needed.

Salt is found in a lot of the food we eat, such as chips.

Sodium is essential to us, but 40% of our body's energy is used to pump it around.

The food industry uses salt to preserve and flavor food.

Too much salt causes high blood pressure, but too little salt causes cramp.

We have better salt supplies than you. We will now become rich and powerful. Your empire will decline.

We'll destroy your salt supplies and then you'll be defeated.

### CHIP INGREDIENTS

dehydrated potatoes, vegetable oil, corn starch, wheat starch, flavorings, salt

### NUTRITION INFORMATION

| Typical values | per 100 g | GDA* |
|---|---|---|
| Energy | 2,211 kj (531 kcal) | 2,000 kcal |
| Protein | 4.5 g | 75 g |
| Carbohydrates | 49 g | 230 g |
| Fat | 35 g | 70 g |
| Fibre | 3.6 g | 24 g |
| Sodium | 0.67 g | 2.5 g |

*Guideline Daily Amount for Adult Women

*Table SALT is sodium*

# Salt mining

Seawater contains sodium and chlorine, which give it the salty taste, making it undrinkable. When seawater evaporates by the Sun's heat, deposits of salt remain. Over time, the salt beds become buried under rock, and the salt has to be mined.

Evaporated seawater leaves vast areas of salt deposits, called salt flats.

Salt flats are another source of salt for people.

200 million tons of salt are mined per year.

*There's more than a pinch of salt here!*

## Salt trade

Many ports and towns grew rapidly due to the trade of salt. Timbuktu in Mali, West Africa, had a huge salt market, and Liverpool in England became a thriving port, exporting salt from the Cheshire salt mines.

*with chlorine.*

### Neon lamps
Pieces of sodium metal are in neon-filled street lights, which use less electricity than other street lights and shine through mist and fog.

### Baking
A sodium compound called bicarbonate of soda is used in cooking to boost the amount of carbon dioxide, which makes the food taste lighter.

### Soaps and detergents
Sodium soaps are often made with caustic soda to produce a hard lather for removing the grime.

### Deicing roads
Salt reduces the freezing point of water. In cold weather, salt is spread onto the roads to prevent melting from snow or water from forming ice.

### Putting out fire
Fire extinguishers contain sodium. It is used in the chemical process that causes a jet of water or foam to spurt out.

### More and more uses:
Sodium compounds are used in many industries, such as glass and dye manufacture. Sodium is also in the gas that goes into the air bags in cars.

*Calcium*

**Over time**, billions and billions of sea creatures have lived and died. Packed with calcium, their bodies have crushed down and fossilized and turned into rocks, such as limestone and gypsum. This has happened to such an extent that calcium is the **fifth** most abundant element on **Earth**.

**White cliffs**
Over billions of years, the crushed remains of dead sea creatures at the bottom of the oceans gradually formed limestone (a compound of calcium, carbon, and oxygen). Some limestone, while still fairly soft, was lifted above sea level by the Earth's movements to form hills and cliffs. That's where we find chalk—a form of limestone.

is a silver-white, *soft metal*. In nature, calcium is always found joined with *other ELEMENTS*.

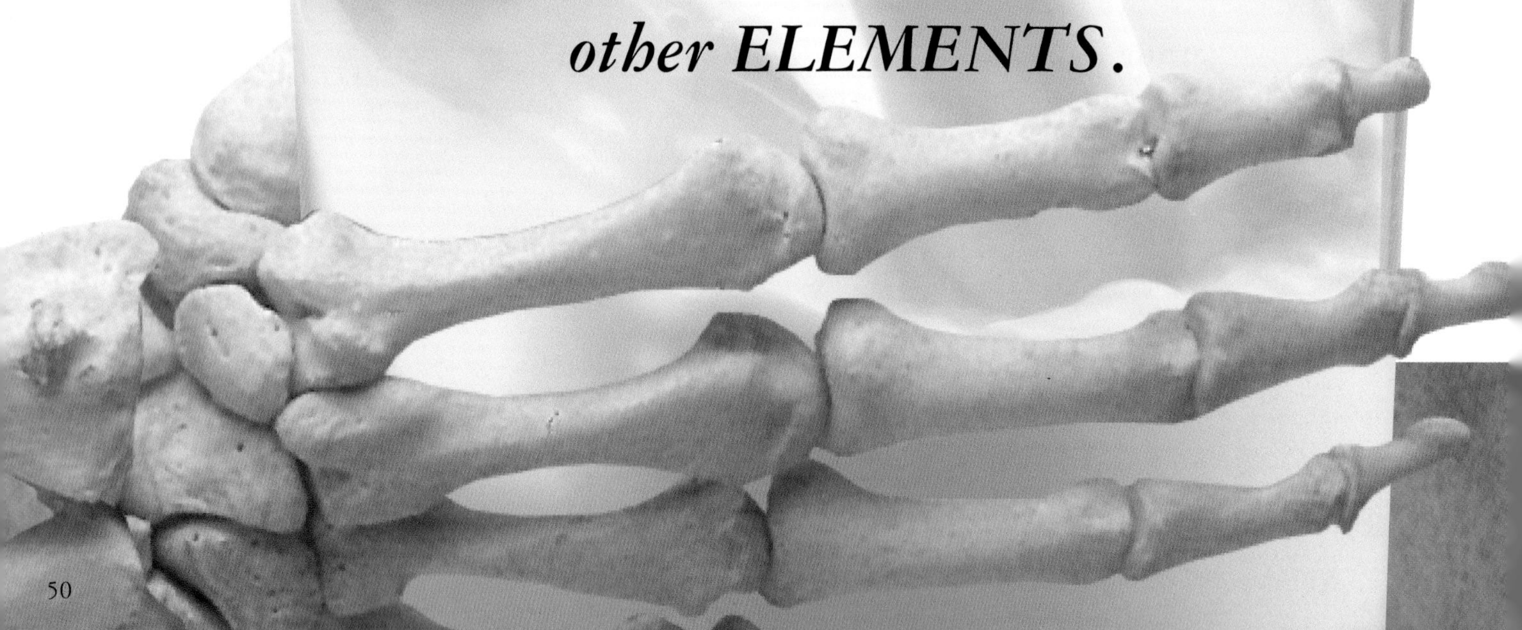

## Living bones

Calcium is the most abundant metal in the human body since it's the main element stored in bones and teeth. It has five vital functions, keeping our cells, muscles, nerves, blood, and hormones working properly. The cells in our bones make sure there's enough calcium in our blood to do all these functions. If the levels in our blood are low, calcium is taken from our bones and replaced later when levels are high again.

*Calcium keeps my teeth and bones strong.*

### Carving out caves

Some calcium, such as limestone, dissolves in mild acidic rainwater, making "hard" water. Over millions of years, this water carves out huge caves, and drips have formed stalactites and stalagmites.

### Spectacular coral

Living in warm, shallow seas, coral contains a crystallized form of a calcium compound. Tiny animals, called polyps, build these chalky shelters in many amazing shapes and colors around their soft bodies.

### Limescale

Hard water, which contains calcium, is good for us to drink. But it reduces the effectiveness of soaps and detergents and leaves deposits on heated appliances, such as tea kettles.

### Stone and mortar

Many buildings would not exist without calcium. It's in the cement and plaster for building walls. Limestone makes great building stones, and marble, a harder form, makes stunning buildings, including the iconic Taj Mahal in India.

*The cells in our bones are constantly broken down and reconstructed.*

*Children, pregnant women, and the elderly need extra calcium to grow new bone.*

*Calcium-rich foods include dairy products, egg yolks, and sardines.*

Each year, about 2,000 tons but over 120 million of calcium metal is produced, tons of limestone is dug out.

# Magnesium

Lightweight but TOUGH, magnesium is a silvery-white shiny metal that burns in air with a dazzlingly white flame.

The **7th** most abundant metal on Earth.

*Magnesium is the fourth most abundant element in our bodies and is needed for more than 300 body processes.*

Leaves appear green as magnesium in the leaves does not absorb the Sun's green rays.

*We get magnesium by eating green plants.*

The **red and BLUE** rays are taken into the leaves.

*I'm from Magnesia in Greece. This element is named after this area.*

The Sun's rays include the colors red, blue, and green.

## Magnesium is essential

for all *green plants.* It's in their *leaves,* where it CAPTURES the *Sun's energy,* which is needed for making the *plants' food.*

## Lightweight

High-tech racing bikes have a frame made from a single piece of magnesium with no nuts and bolts. They are light, strong, and, most importantly, speedy.

## Long-lasting

As a light and long-lasting metal, magnesium is used for making the casings of many everyday objects, such as lawn mowers, power tools, and cameras.

## High performance

The wheels of sports cars may also be made from magnesium. These mag wheels give better performance than heavier steel or aluminum wheels.

## Heat resistant

Since magnesium has a high melting point and resists heat and fire, it is used in bricks for fireplaces and in fireproof materials.

## Epsom salts

In 1618, a farmer walking across Epsom Common, England, saw that thirsty cattle were not drinking from a pool of water. He found the water tasted bitter, but healed rashes. The water contained magnesium with sulfur—used today as a cure for indigestion.

## Recyclable

440,000 tons (400,000 metric tons) of magnesium are produced each year, but demand for the metal is increasing. Therefore, some magnesium is being recycled, saving energy.

*It might be good for you, but it tastes gross!*

# IRON

We're living on an *enormous* lump of iron—*Earth.* The *middle* of the Earth is almost ALL iron and there's lots on the *surface*, too, which is handy since we have many uses for it.

## Meteorites

are mostly iron. The ancients used them to make the first iron objects.

> Iron gives red blood cells their color.

*Iron is stored in our **blood** cells, liver, and other tissues.*

*The iron compound* that makes the soil *on Mars*

*It's a silvery, pliable, heavy metal with nerves of steel.*

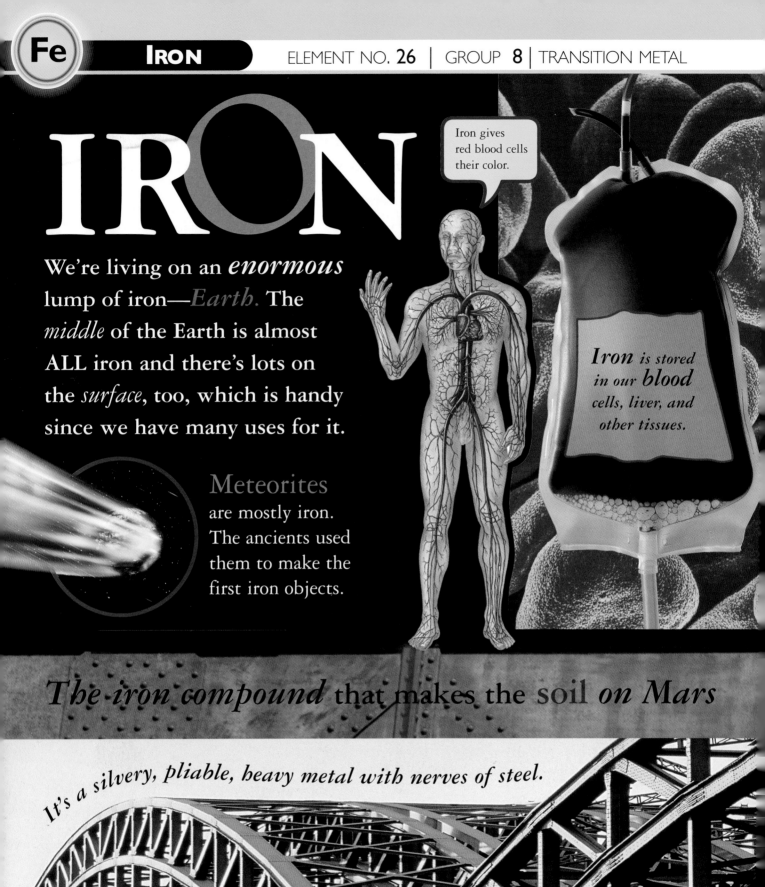

# Postmen

Iron is needed throughout our bodies, but essentially in our blood. The iron atoms in blood carry oxygen from our lungs to our heart and brain, and then take carbon dioxide back to our lungs to breathe out, like tiny elemental postmen.

*It's good to eat a variety of **iron-rich foods**, such as beef.*

## Most-used metal

Iron is the most used of all the metals because it's very hard. But first it has to be extracted from iron ore. From steel in the hulls of ships and cast iron in pipes, to stainless steel in cutlery and wrought iron gates, iron is the main element found in many objects you see and use every day.

## OBSERVATIONS

### Rust disgust

When iron is mixed with water and oxygen, rust is formed. This corrodes (eats away) iron objects, such as the exhaust on a car. So make sure your iron toys don't get wet!

### Magnetic personality

Things made from iron are attracted to magnets. Try picking up paper clips, nails, or even the crumbs in cereal boxes with a magnet. They all contain iron atoms and become magnetic, too.

*RED* is the same as the rust *on old bikes on Earth.*

# Elements in color

ORPIMENT
(arsenic and sulfur)

The ancient Egyptians used many colors to decorate their temples and tombs. Some of the minerals they used, such as orpiment, were poisonous.

LAPIS LAZULI
(clay [aluminum, silicon] with sulfur)

They created the first artificial paints using minerals, such as lapis lazuli, which was crushed to make blue paint.

REALGAR
(arsenic and sulfur)

For red pigments, the ancients crushed the mineral realgar, but this contained ARSENIC, so it is no longer used.

MALACHITE
(copper and carbon compound)

The mineral malachite was also crushed to make green paint.

## What elements are

Aluminum

Calcium

Titanium

Iron

Oxygen

Selenium

## Open a paint can and you'll

...contained some harmful elements.

TITANIUM or ZINC is used to make white paints.

CADMIUM, ZINC, and SULFUR make the color cadmium yellow.

SILICON, ALUMINUM, or IRON with OXYGEN created the yellow ochers used by the cavemen.

COPPER COMPOUNDS are used to make blue paint.

COBALT and ALUMINUM make the color cobalt blue.

COBALT COMPOUNDS are used to make purple paint.

are quite new, replacing those that contained...

FOR A MASTERPIECE, DAB ON SOME CADMIUM, A STROKE OF COPPER, SPLASHES OF COBALT, STREAKS OF ZINC,

**Since cavemen** used the *clay soil* to *draw* on the walls of their caves, artists have **crushed** many rocks and minerals to create *colors* for their paintings. The search continues for the elements that will provide the best, most long-lasting colors.

## in your paint can?

Carbon

Copper

Cobalt

Silicon

Sulfur

Cadmium

Zinc

still find some of the original earth colors used by the cavemen. Some paints were used by the artists of the past, but other paints

**COPPER COMPOUNDS** create the green paints.

**ALUMINUM, SILICON, or IRON** with **OXYGEN** have created earth greens since the cavemen.

**IRON or MANGANESE** with **OXYGEN** have made the browns called sienna and umber since cavemen times.

**CADMIUM, SULFUR, and SELENIUM** make the color cadmium red.

**IRON** with **OXYGEN** has created the gold colors used since the cavemen.

**CARBON, CALCIUM, and IRON** with **OXYGEN** make the bone black paint.

The ancients crushed the mineral stibnite for their black paint. They even used it as an eye liner. But **antimony** is toxic.

STIBNITE
(antimony and sulfur)

The mineral cerusite was crushed to make white paint. But it contained the toxic element **lead,** and so it is no longer used.

CERUSITE
(lead and carbon)

Medieval painters used the mineral cinnabar to create their red paints. This contained the toxic element **mercury.**

CINNABAR
(sulfur and mercury)

Medieval painters crushed the mineral azurite to make another shade of blue. Making the various colors took time.

AZURITE
(copper and carbon compound)

BRIGHTEN WITH TITANIUM, SHADE WITH CARBON, AND ADD A TOUCH OF SELENIUM.

# Explosive elements

Let's celebrate! Nowhere do we use the elements to more spectacular effect than in fireworks.

Whizzzzzzzzzzzz!

Purple—potassium

Blue—copper compounds

Green—barium compounds

White—aluminum

Red—strontium or lithium salts

Orange—calcium compounds

Yellow—sodium compounds

Whizzzzzzz!

## SPECIAL EFFECTS

Certain sodium compounds provide the whistling sound and glitter effect.

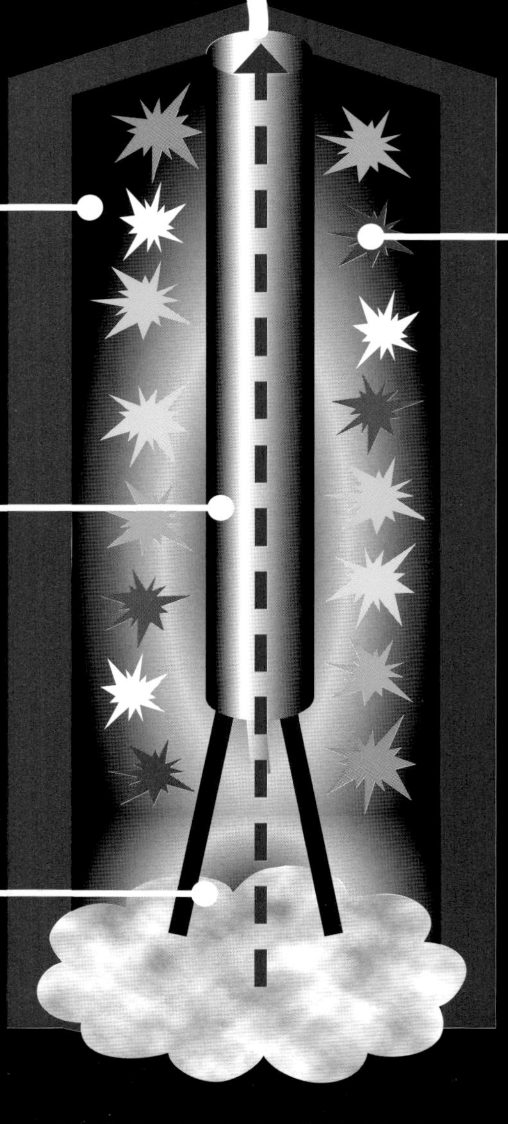

## FOR *SPARKLE*:

### Pea-sized stars

Once ignited, these carefully arranged shaped sparklers will burn with a bright shower of sparks in the night sky.

CONTAINS:

The elements that make the colors and special effects, plus...

### an oxidizer

a potassium compound containing oxygen, which makes things burn faster and hotter.

### metal flakes

aluminum, iron, steel, zinc, or magnesium to increase brightness and sparkle.

## BANG!
### BANG!
### BANG!

*Wheeeeeeeeee!*

## FOR THE BANG:

### Black powder

When the powder inside the rocket explodes, it causes the outside of the stars to ignite and zoom off in all directions.

CONTAINS:

### charcoal
(carbon)

### sulfur

### potassium
and nitrogen

*These are the same ingredients as gunpowder, but the amounts are changed for rocket fuel.*

# SILVER

This *beautiful shiny metal* has often had to play second fiddle to **gold**.

Silver's symbol Ag comes from the Latin word *argentums*. (Also the word used to name "Argentina," in South America.)

### Refined

In the past, silver was extracted from other metals. Metal was placed in a shallow cup called a cupel and heated under a strong gust of air. This process removed the other metals, leaving globules of liquid silver.

## Worn-out coins

For thousands of years, silver coins were used as currency. However, silver wears away easily, so it's no longer used.

*1.2 miles (2 km) long.*

**STERLING SILVER**
A LITTLE COPPER IS ADDED TO SILVER TO MAKE IT HARDER AND PREVENT IT FROM WEARING AWAY.

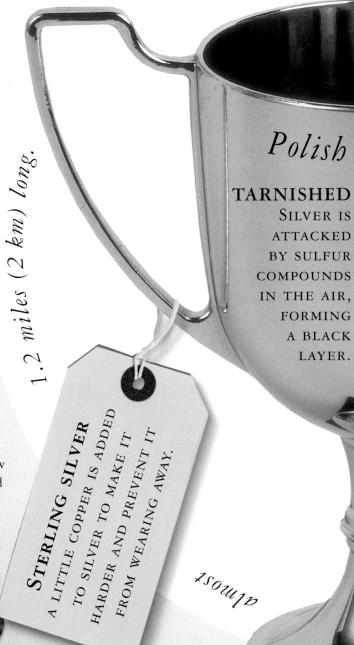

*Polish*

**TARNISHED** SILVER IS ATTACKED BY SULFUR COMPOUNDS IN THE AIR, FORMING A BLACK LAYER.

*almost*

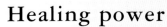

SILVER
2ND

*the silver!*

### SHINY
THEREFORE, SILVER OBJECTS NEED TO BE CLEANED REGULARLY.

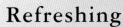

$\frac{1}{25}$ *oz* (*1g*) *of silver can be beaten into a thin wire*

## Healing power
Silver kills off many bacteria and viruses, so particles are added to some wound dressings to prevent infections.

## Electric
As the best conductor of heat and electricity, silver is used in many electrical and electronic devices to make and break electric circuits precisely.

## Sparkle
Shiny and easily molded, silver is often found as part of jewelry. However, to prevent it wearing away, copper is added. (Usually about 20% of silver jewelry is in fact copper.)

## Fine dining
In the most chic restaurants, tables are set with gleaming silver-plated cutlery. Waiters and waitresses serve the food in a particular way called "silver service."

## Refreshing
Smelly feet are a thing of the past thanks to silver fibers in some socks. The silver kills off the bacteria that cause the smell from sweaty feet.

## Light sensitive
As silver is sensitive to light, silver compounds are coated onto the film of x-rays and photographic prints to make the images.

## Sterilizing
Water can be sterilized and made safe to drink and swim in by adding silver salts. This was known by the ancients, who threw silver coins into wells that they drank from.

# Mirror, mirror, on the wall,
what makes the glass reflective? SILVER!

# Gold

This soft, yellow metal has been highly prized since prehistoric times. IS THIS BECAUSE its gorgeous glow never tarnishes, or because it'll never crumble in air or water? Whatever the reason, this element excites people like no other.

*Tutankhamun*
*1361–1352 BCE*

## King bling

Objects made from gold have been used to display wealth and power for thousands of years. Grains or nuggets of gold were sifted from streams and riverbeds. The ancient Egyptians collected loads from the Nile River—enough to make the amazing gold artifacts found in the pharaoh Tutankhamun's tomb.

## Eureka!

The king of Syracuse in Sicily had a new crown. He wanted Archimedes to check that it was made from pure gold as he had requested—but without damaging it. Biting into it to see if teeth marks were left on the soft metal was not an option!

*Gold or not gold? That is the question.*

*Archimedes*
*257–212 BCE*

Archimedes noticed how the water level rose when he sat down to take a bath. "Eureka!" he shouted—he had found how to solve the puzzle. He weighed the crown, and then lowered it into an urn of water, taking note of how far the water level went up. Then he did this to the same weight of pure gold… and less water was displaced. So the crown could not have been pure gold! The goldsmith confessed that he had added silver, which had reduced the crown's density.

*Not gold!*

## Golden touch

Many early dabblers in chemistry, the alchemists, believed they could make the philosophers' stone that would turn metals such as lead into gold.

*Mount Erebus in Antarctica spews out gold dust in its continuous volcanic eruptions.*

The 18 carat World Cup soccer trophy is 75% solid gold.

## Pure gold

The amount of gold in an object is measured in carats. Pure gold is 24 carats. A carat was originally a unit of weight based on the carob seed or bean, and it was used by ancient merchants in the Middle East. Hallmarking objects with their caratage was first done at Goldsmith's Hall, England, in the 14th century.

## Gold rush

Driven by the desire for gold, people throughout history have gone to great lengths to obtain it. 16th century Spanish explorers killed for it in Central and South America. In the 19th century, people joined the gold rush in the hope of becoming wealthy by finding some in a stream. Even today, gold is mined to depths of 10,000 ft (3,000 m) in South Africa.

# Gold is used for
teeth fillings, electrical circuit boards, space satellites, coins, and jewelry.

Gold's **chemical** symbol, **Au,** comes from the **Latin** word *aurum,* meaning "glow of sunrise."

Gold is the most workable metal. It can be hammered into incredibly thin sheets called gold leaf. A piece the size of a grain of rice will cover 10 sq ft (1 square meter)! Its many uses include covering ornaments and decorating buildings.

# At *home* with

Everything in our homes—from the *walls* and *windows* to the *curtains* and *cupboards*—

## Electronics

Switch on, power up, type out, scroll down, click send... Which elements give us this power at our fingertips?

- **SEMICONDUCTORS:** Controlling the flow of electricity, semiconductors, such as silicon, are key components of electrical devices.

- **CIRCUIT BREAKERS:** Layers of conductive elements, such as copper, silver, and gold, connect and disconnect the electricity.

- **IMAGE MAKERS:** Curved screens molded from glass (silicon plus other elements) are coated with colored phosphors. These are the rare earth elements that emit light to create the images.

- **LIGHT, STRONG CASING:** Aluminum or steel (iron) are ideal to protect the components inside.

STAR ELEMENTS: (Si) (Cu) (Ag) (Eu)

## Essentials

24/7, we use elements to help us do everyday tasks.

- **POWER SOURCES:** Lightweight, rechargeable nickel-cadmium batteries and heat-resistant tungsten in lightbulbs power up our lives.
- **LONG-LASTING:** Stainless steel (iron, carbon, chromium, and nickel) is used for pans and cutlery.
- **LIFESAVING:** Americium is used to make smoke detectors work.

STAR ELEMENTS:

(Ni) (Cd) (W)
(Fe) (C) (Cr)

## Materials

What's in the bricks and mortar, pipes and cables, windows and doors, tiles and flooring?

- **STRONG and DURABLE:** Gypsum rock (calcium and sulfur compound) is used to form walls and ceilings.

- **INSULATORS:** Copper or PVC plastic (chlorine compound) pipes keep hot water hot and cold water cold.

- **HEAT RESISTANT:** Argon or krypton gas between the glass (silicon, calcium) windows prevents heat from escaping.

- **WATER-RESISTANT:** Kaolinite clay (aluminum and silicon) is used for ceramic tiles, toilets, and worktops.

STAR ELEMENTS: (Ca) (S) (Cu) (Cl) (Ar) (Al)

# the elements

is made from one or more **ELEMENTS**. But why are these elements so useful to us?

## Cleaning

Scrubbing the dishes, washing our clothes, cleaning our muddy hands, and disinfecting the worktops and toilets would be much harder without the help of elements.

- **KILLS GERMS:** The disinfectant chlorine bleach kills viruses and bacteria that are harmful to us and cleans white clothes, keeping them white.
- **CLEANS and SHINES:** Sodium salts make hard soaps for removing tough grease, while potassium salts make softer soaps for hand-washing.

STAR ELEMENTS:

## Medical

Open up the medicine cabinet or first aid kit and discover the healing power of the elements. They are the cures and treatments for our cuts and bruises, our pains and aches, and our upset tummies and nasty viruses.

- **ANTIBIOTICS:** Penicillin (sulfur) is one of many medicines that destroys harmful bacteria.
- **LOTIONS:** Zinc ointments soothe irritations on our skin.
- **LAXATIVES:** Magnesium soothes digestive discomforts.

STAR ELEMENTS:

## Appliances

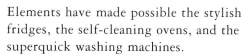

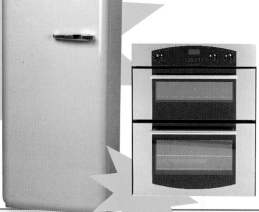

Elements have made possible the stylish fridges, the self-cleaning ovens, and the superquick washing machines.

- **STYLE:** The long-lasting, brilliant white coating on today's appliances are a nontoxic titanium compound.
- **HEAT:** Even when red hot, nickel and chromium wires are not damaged, so are used in toasters and ovens.

- **SELF-CLEANS:** A cerium compound coated on an oven wall prevents the build up of burning drips and grime.

STAR ELEMENTS:

# SAND

Take a pile of sand (silicon), mix it with lime (calcium) and soda ash (carbon, sodium), and heat to a very high temperature.

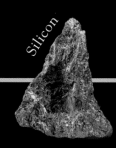

Silicon

# AIR

Collect some air and cool it to a temperature of -303°F (-186°C). Extract the liquid argon.

# ROCKS

Mine scheelite or wolframite and bring to the surface. Crush and mill the ore to release the tungsten mineral crystals for separation.

Scheelite

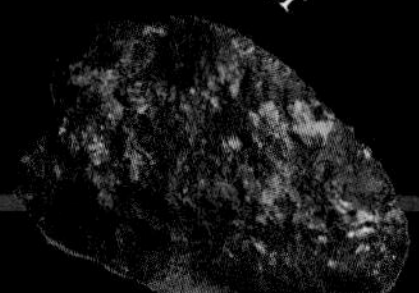

# ELEMENTS OF *light*

*Fluorescent lightbulbs used today are energy-saving and longer-lasting. Why? Because the elements used have been specially chosen to turn electricity efficiently into light.*

Cinnabar

Crush cinnabar and heat it to 1,100°F (593°C) in a kiln to release the mercury as vapors. Cool the kiln to collect the mercury.

Process monazite with caustic soda. Remove the rare earth metals and separate by passing between an oil and a water layer over 60 times.

Monazite

The rare earth metals used are europium, which emits blue light; lanthanum, cerium, and terbium, which emit green light; and yttrium and europium, which emit red light.

## GLASS

### Glass bulb

As the molten liquid cools, shape into glass. Blow the molten glass into a bulb-shaped mold.

## ARGON

### Stabilizer

Insert the stable, colorless argon gas into the bulb. Argon makes the lamp easier to start as it does not react with any of the other elements inside the bulb.

## TUNGSTEN

### Electrode

Twist the dull gray powder of pure tungsten into a wire to make the electrode, which emits the electric current.

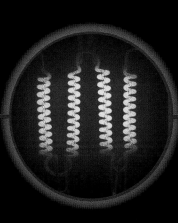

## MERCURY

Mercury

### Energy

Insert a tiny piece of mercury into the bulb. The electricity causes the mercury to vaporize and this releases ultraviolet (invisible light) energy that strikes the phosphors.

## PHOSPHOR

### White light

Coat the inside of the bulb with the tricolored phosphors (rare earth compounds). Excited by the ultraviolet energy, the phosphors fluoresce. The three colors combine to create a visible white light.

How many *elements* are needed to make a LIGHTBULB? Lots!

# TOXIC

## Beware of the infamous elements—

Convulsions, madness, pains, insanity, loss of hair, paralysis, and even death can be caused by exposure to some of the elements.

Turn sick of feeling depressed

### ANTIMONY

The early death of the composer Mozart at age 35 is thought to be due to taking too much of the antimony compound given to him by his doctor for his depression.

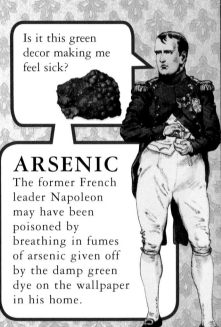

Is it this green decor making me feel sick?

### ARSENIC

The former French leader Napoleon may have been poisoned by breathing in fumes of arsenic given off by the damp green dye on the wallpaper in his home.

**DANGER: DO NOT CROSS    DANGER: DO NOT CROSS    DANGER: DO**

I'll make gold, even if it kills me!

### MERCURY

Many dabblers in alchemy, such as the scientist Isaac Newton, had mercury poisoning. Other people were given mercury as a cure, but it killed them instead.

### PHOSPHORUS

In the 19th century, matches were made using white phosphorus. Matchmakers suffered from "phossy jaw" as the element slowly ate away their jaw bones.

### RADIOACTIVE ELEMENTS

In 2006, polonium gained international notoriety when it was used for the mysterious fatal poisoning of the Russian dissident Alexander Litvinenko in London.

# ELEMENTS!

## contact with them will cause certain death.

### CADMIUM

A painful weakening disease known as Itai-Itai ("ouch-ouch") in Japan was caused by eating rice grown on land contaminated with high levels of cadmium.

### CARBON

Some simple carbon compounds can be extremely dangerous, such as the gas carbon monoxide, caused when fuel does not burn properly. Cyanide is also lethal, and fish are even more sensitive to it than humans.

Port wine was kept in lead crystal decanters

### LEAD

The biologist Charles Darwin was one of many wealthy people who suffered from gout (swollen joints). They had high levels of lead in their blood, possibly from drinking the port wine containing traces of lead.

**CROSS    DANGER: DO NOT CROSS    DANGER: DO NOT CROSS**

YEE-HAH!

### SELENIUM

The Great Plains of the US are rich in selenium. Cowboys knew that if their herds ate the vetch (a type of plant), the animals would go insane and stagger around.

### THALLIUM

The mystery writer Agatha Christie, who worked as a pharmacist, used thallium as the murderer's poison in her novel *The Pale Horse*. The first clue of its use came from the hair loss suffered by the victims.

## Too much of most elements is toxic.

# Aluminum

is a shiny, silvery, *soft metal*.

It's **malleable**, it doesn't **rust,** it's light and tough, it conducts electricity, and it reflects heat and light. So, it's extremely useful.

Its name is taken from *alumen,* the Latin name for the mineral alum, which contains aluminum. Alum has been used since ancient times to fix natural dyes to fabrics.

**95%** = The energy saved *by recycling*

Lots of *aluminum*

can be found in **soil,**

Tea

so plants absorb it,

especially tea bushes.

The most **abundant** metal on the Earth's surface.

It's reflective like a mirror.

Ruby    Sapphire

Topaz

## GEMSTONES

Aluminum is a key element in a number of precious and very beautiful stones. Sapphire, ruby, topaz, turquoise, and jade all contain aluminum, although often it's other elements that give them their amazing colors.

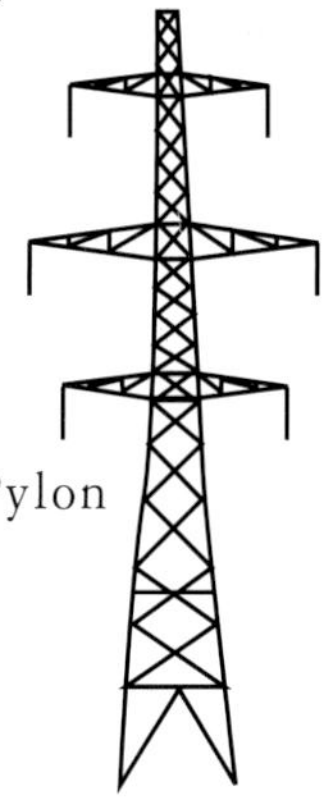

Pylon

As a good conductor of **electricity**, aluminium is ideal for power cables.

Packaging.

## TRANSPORTATION

Boats, car bodies, motor engines, and aircraft parts all use aluminum for its lightweight and strong protective qualities.

Mast

Aluminum foil

*Every year, 22 million tons (20 million metric tons) of aluminum is produced worldwide from its ore. About the same amount is **recycled**.*

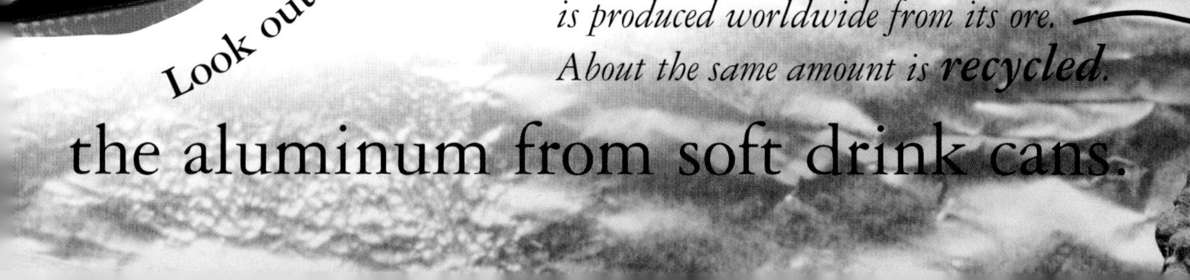

Look out for it in food and drink

the aluminum from soft drink cans.

# SiLiCON

Making sandcastles wouldn't be possible without silicon.

## Ever heard of *silicon*? How about *sand*?

Silicon with oxygen makes sand—and there is a LOT of sand in the world.

Sand covers over half of the Earth's surface.

**Ultrapure silicon** makes blue-gray, metallic-looking crystals.

### Choked to death
Inhalation of fine silica causes the lung condition called silicosis. Asbestos, a silicon compound, was once used for building materials and insulation, but causes lung cancer.

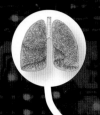

## Glass

When heated at high temperatures around 2,552°F (1,400°C), sand becomes natural green-colored glass. When other elements are added, the glass can become different colors.

## Quartz crystals

Crystals of pure silicon with oxygen vibrate precisely when connected to an electric current. These are used in atomic clocks to keep the exact time.

## Minerals and gems

There's a great variety of minerals and gems containing silicon, such as smooth, flaky talc used for skincare, and sparkling opals, rhinestones, and amethysts.

## Implants

The oily-feeling and very versatile silicones have many uses, which include cosmetic implants, skin and hair gels, and rubber hoses.

## Silicon chips

Personal computers were made possible by using ultrapure silicon to make microchips. As the semiconductor of electricity for electronic devices, silicon is part of our everyday lives for learning and communicating with each other.

*Watch out!*

Sponges use silicon to make their skeletons.

Nettle stings are tiny needles of silica.

It's like being pierced by minute pieces of glass.

**SILICON VALLEY**

*OUCH! That nettle stings!*

# SULFUR

## ... is a very fine yellow powder.

### It stinks when sulfur is burned in air.

**Known since ancient times, sulfur was called brimstone by the English.** The threat of "hellfire and brimstone" was used to frighten people into being good.

## Stink bloom

One of the world's largest flowers, the Titan alum lily blooms impressively once every four years. But it produces a rotting-fish smell due to its sulfur compounds.

A certain species of bee loves this smell and is attracted to the flower, pollinating the plant.

*Skunk odor contains* **THREE** *sulfur compounds.*

## SMELLY USES

### Pulp to paper
In paper mills, sulfur compounds are used to break down the strong fibers of the wood pulp and to bleach the paper.

### Fermentation
Sulfur is added to the fermenting process during winemaking. It kills any undesirable yeasts in the wine, allowing the good yeasts to multiply.

### Vulcanization
Heating sulfur with natural rubber makes rubber very flexible and weatherproof. This process is called "vulcanization" and rubber made like this makes superb car tires.

*Underground deposits of sulfur are melted into liquid and forced to the surface. Once it reaches the air, the sulfur hardens again. That's when we pick it up to use.*

# VENTS OF LIFE
Sulfur occurs naturally near volcanoes, including in hot water vents in the oceans. The first, simplest forms of life on Earth may have begun beneath the oceans, surviving on water and the sulfur gas emitted from these volcanic vents.

### Destructive
When burning coal and heating oil, sulfur is released into the atmosphere. It falls back to Earth as part of acid rain, which attacks trees and so destroys forests.

# ESSENTIAL
Sulfur is not all bad! It's essential to all living things since it is part of proteins. The sulfur bond in the protein keratin gives strength to our skin, hair, and nails.

When sulfur is heated, it melts to form bright yellow crystals.

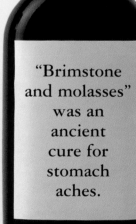

"Brimstone and molasses" was an ancient cure for stomach aches.

### Antibiotics
Penicillin, a medicine that kills harmful bacteria, is a sulfur compound.

# Icky, rotten eggs?
## No, *it's sulfur with hydrogen.*

Sulfur is added to gas supplies, so the compound will smell if there is a leak.

*A heavy, silvery metal.*

# QUiCK silveR

*Fish from the oceans contain mercury.*

Known since 1500 BCE.

**Since** ancient times, **mercury** has been surrounded by mystery. The liquid metal is easily obtained and fascinating to look at— no wonder people thought it was magical. It's found in every living thing and, therefore, in every mouthful of food we eat.

*But* BEWARE!

MERCURY EXPANDS, OR GETS BIGGER, WHEN HEATED. AS THE TEMPERATURE RISES, SO DOES THE MERCURY.

# Once *valued* as a medicine...

## Finding mercury

Mercury is extracted by heating cinnabar, a red mineral. This is found around the world, but most abundantly in Spain, Russia, and China.

All forms of mercury are dangerous, however, methylmercury is the most poisonous. This can be found in microorganisms in chemically polluted waters. It becomes more harmful as it passes along the food chain to the fish that people eat.

# Mercury is the heaviest *liquid* **element.**

### KILL OR CURE

Since ancient times, mercury has been widely used in industry, medicines, and agriculture, despite the knowledge that it was toxic. In the hat trade, workers were poisoned by the mercury compounds used to make the felt and suffered from hallucinations. It was not until the late 1950s that scientists recommended the restricted use of mercury.

I'm as mad as a hatter.

## ONCE USED IN:

Thermometers,

felt-making,

and gilding with gold and silver.

## NOW USED IN:

Dental fillings,

button cell batteries,

and fluorescent lights (in tiny amounts).

*It's also called quicksilver because it's quick moving and silvery!*

## now *proven* to be a deadly toxin.

Chlorine is the C in PVC (poly vinyl chloride), used to make window frames, garden furniture, and bottles.

# CHLORINE

## CHOKING
In 1915 during World War I, chlorine gas was used against the British troops with devastating results. The gas is very toxic, affecting eyes and lungs, and causing death.

**TOILETS**

## BLEACHING
Chlorine is a main element in bleaching and cleaning products. It can remove ink from recycled paper and is ideal in paint-strippers and pesticides.

Chlorine

Cl

Viruses and bacteria are quickly

Chlorine kills off waterborne diseases, so it's used to make water safe to drink and swim in.

**When** **chlorine** *joins* with another element, it becomes **a** chloride. This is *stable* and relatively *nontoxic*, such as sodium chloride, otherwise known as salt.

Named from the Greek word *chloros*, meaning "pale green."

# As a dense, smelly, greenish-yellow gas,
chlorine is extremely reactive and dangerous, although its destructive properties can also be useful to us.

## AIR POLLUTION
Today, the use of CFCs (chlorofluorocarbons) is strictly controlled, since chlorine atoms can destroy the ozone layer.

*Aerosol cans used to contain CFCs.*

## WATER POLLUTION
Chlorine products washed into rivers and streams can harm the wildlife and the environment.

# destroyed by chlorine products.

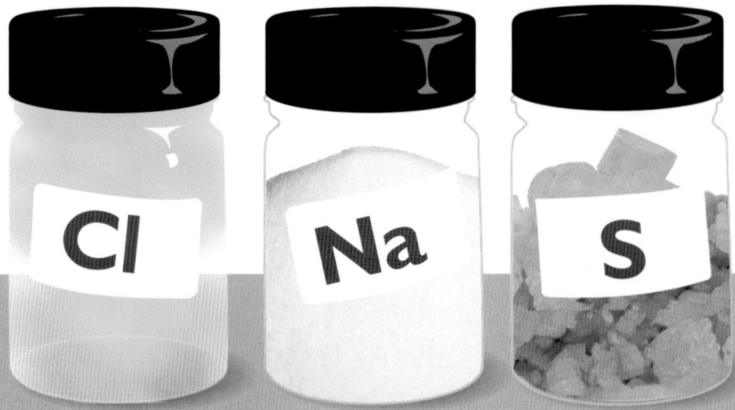

**Cl** **Na** **S**

STIFF

HARD

*soft*

FlexiBle

# DESIGNER

## By knowing the properties of elements, scientists can combine or manipulate them to create the ideal products.

Since prehistoric times, people have used materials because they had the properties they needed. Today, designers think about the properties they would like to have for a product, such as "waterproof" or "elastic," and scientists create new materials with just these properties.

### NANOTECHNOLOGY

This new technology involves working with the atoms and molecules of materials. At this size, measured in nanometers, scientists have found that the materials often work better and have added benefits.

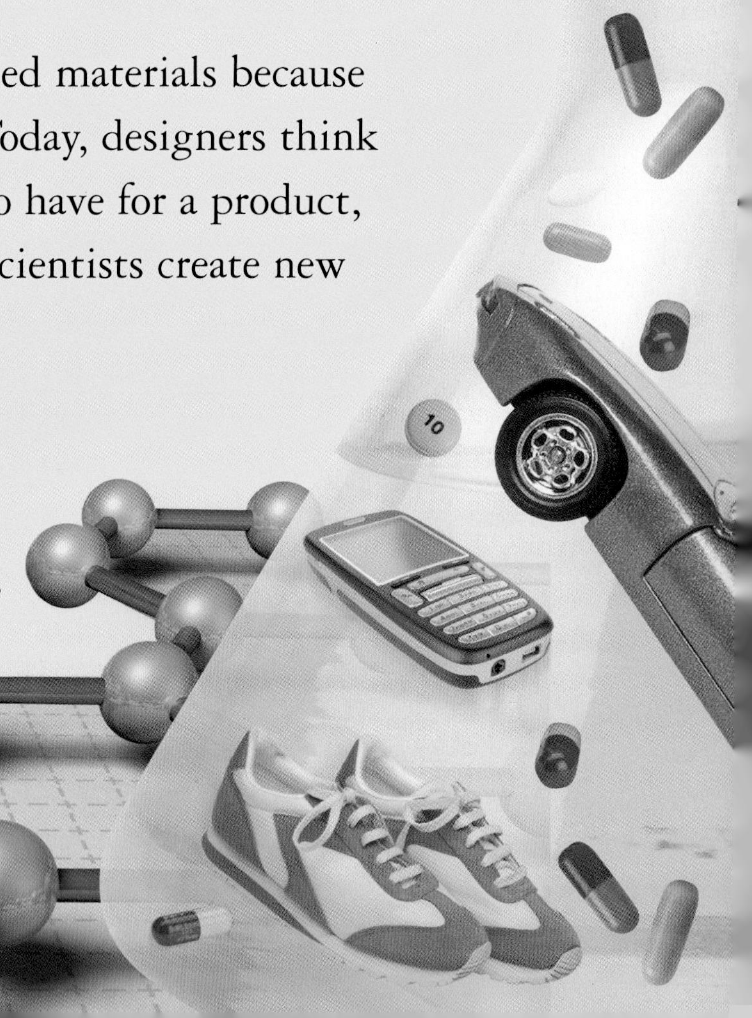

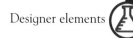

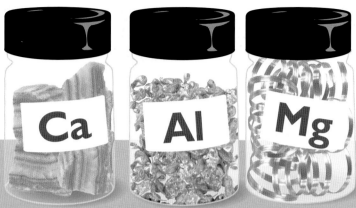

*Cheap* **STRONG** *Eco-friendly*

# ELEMENTS

*Creating new materials by manipulating the elements can make inventions even better.*

## Combinations

New materials can be created by carefully rearranging existing materials. For example, carbon fibers are very strong but inflexible. But set these in plastic and you have a flexible material four times stronger than steel, as used in tennis rackets.

## Small but clever

Sunblock made from a titanium compound once looked like face paint because the large particles reflected light. But, use instead the nano-sized particles of the same compound that are too small to reflect light, and the sunblock is now invisible.

## That's smart!

Smart materials can sense and react to changes in their environment. For example, superelastic glasses made from nickel and titanium can return to their original shape if bent.

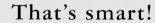

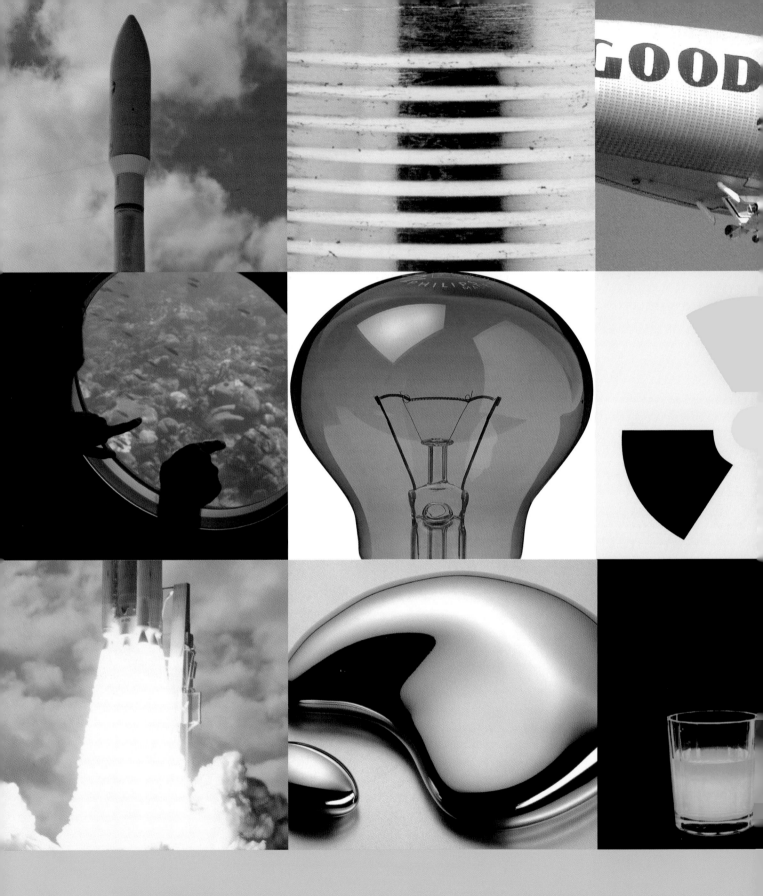

*What's in a* **NAME** ?

# " Did you know...

**Scandium** is put into baseball bats to increase their **striking power**.

**Bismuth** is used to make lipstick **shiny**.

The **fake snow** on film sets is made using **boron**.

In fact, we humans have found a use, or many uses, for EVERY SINGLE natural element.

Oh, except for **lutetium**.
Well, it is the most expensive metal in the world. "

*I'm out of my depth.*

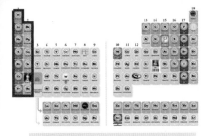

# Alkali metals and

### 1 HYDROGEN **H**

The name comes from the ancient Greek *hydor* and *genes,* meaning "water-forming." Many of its uses are as natural gas, as liquid hydrogen, as water, and as acids.

### 3 LITHIUM **Li**

The name comes from the Greek *lithos,* meaning "stone," because lithium was first discovered in the stone petalite. As the lightest of all metals, lithium is used for aircraft, bicycle frames, and high-speed trains, making them lighter and stronger. Lithium batteries are compact and light, and so are ideal to power many small items, such as wristwatches, pocket calculators, toys, personal stereos, and heart pacemakers. It's used in air-conditioning and also added to make glass resistant to sudden heating or cooling, such as for television tubes.

### 11 SODIUM **Na**

Sodium is named after soda and its symbol comes from Latin *natrium,* meaning "soda." Many of its uses are as a salt, such as in food and detergents, but many chemicals are produced using sodium metal.

### 19 POTASSIUM **K**

The name potassium comes from the medieval word potash, which was plant ash used to flavor and preserve food and as a fertilizer. Its symbol comes from the Latin *kalium,* meaning "potash." Today, potassium is still used in fertilizers. It is also added to glass, making it stronger and more scratch-resistant for use in televisions. Potassium is found in liquid soap and detergents and medicines. In drought areas, potassium (with chlorine) particles are released from flares on the wings of aircraft, causing the clouds to release heavier rainfall. Potassium superoxide is kept in mines, submarines, and space vehicles to maintain sufficient oxygen supplies.

### 37 RUBIDIUM **Rb**

The name comes from the Latin *rubidius,* meaning "deepest red" (ruby), since rubidium turns a flame this color. This element has few uses because it is expensive. It is mostly used for research, but global navigation satellite systems use rubidium-powered atomic clocks. Sometimes rubidium is used to make the purple color in fireworks.

### 55 CESIUM **Cs**

The name comes from the Latin *caseius,* meaning "sky blue," since cesium compounds turn a flame this color. Most cesium-containing minerals are extracted from Bernic Lake in Manitoba, Canada. Cesium is used in making optical glass and other glass can be strengthened when dipped into liquid

cesium salts. Cesium with iodine or fluorine gives off light as it absorbs X-rays, so these compounds are used in medical diagnostics and radiation monitoring. Cesium atoms keep an atomic clock exact. The atoms move back and forth billions of times a second. This clock is used as the standard measure of time because the atoms tell the time to a billionth of a second and will not gain or lose a second in millions of years. Many technologies, such as satellites, cell phones, and television broadcasts, rely on atomic clocks.

### 67 FRANCIUM **Fr**

Named after the country France, francium is intensely radioactive. It is the most unstable of all radioactive elements up to 100 and the second rarest element on Earth. It has the shortest half-life of 22 minutes (the time it takes for half its radioactivity to disappear), which makes it tricky to investigate.

# ALKALINE EARTH METALS

## GROUP 2

*These shiny, silvery-white elements are called alkaline earth metals. They are only found joined with other elements on Earth since they are reactive.*

### 4 BERYLLIUM | Be

Named from *beryllos*, the Greek name for the semiprecious stone beryl, beryllium is a light, strong, but highly poisonous metal. The precious gems emerald and alexandrite contain beryllium with 2% chromium providing the green color. When beryllium is added to copper and nickel, they become better conductors of electricity and heat and have an elastic quality, ideal for making excellent springs and spark-proof tools. Parts of the space shuttle are made with metals containing beryllium.

### 12 MAGNESIUM | Mg

Magnesium was named after Magnesia, a district of Thessaly in Greece. It is the seventh most abundant element on the Earth's surface. As part of the chlorophyll molecule in leaves, magnesium is essential for all green plants. Chlorophyll captures the Sun's energy for making plant food. Magnesium compounds such as "Milk of Magnesia" and Epsom salts are used in medicines to cure digestive problems, as well as sedatives to relax muscles. Some magnesium extracted from minerals is made into heat-resistant bricks for fireplaces and furnaces, as large amounts are difficult to ignite. Magnesium metal is light and long-lasting. When added to 10% aluminum and traces of zinc and manganese, magnesium has improved strength, corrosion resistance, and welding qualities, which are ideal for car bodies, aircraft, lawn mowers, luggage, and power tools. The whole frame of a racing bicycle is made from a cast of pure magnesium. Recycled magnesium is increasingly being used, saving 95% of the energy required to extract it from its ores.

### 20 CALCIUM | Ca

The name comes from the Latin word *calx*, meaning "lime." Lime is one of many calcium compounds—the ancients used lime to make mortar for their buildings. Calcium is one of the most abundant metals on Earth, especially in the form of limestone. Calcium goes into cement, plaster, soil conditioners, and water and sewage treatments. It is found in plaster of Paris used for broken limbs casts, and easily carved alabaster, which is used to make sculptures. Before the widespread use of electricity, lime was used to create a brilliant white light that could be seen for miles. This was used for the flashing lights in lighthouses and also as a shining spotlight for stage performers in theaters. This led to the phrase "to be in the limelight," which means to be center of attention.

### 38 STRONTIUM | Sr

Strontium was named after the village of Strontian in Scotland, where a mineral containing it was first found in a lead mine. Shells of some deep-sea creatures contain this element and stony corals need it to survive, so it is necessary for strontium to be added to the water in aquariums. It is a component of the glass on television screens and visual display units and provides the bright red effects in warning flares.

### 56 BARIUM | Ba

The name comes from the Greek *barys*, meaning heavy. Patients suffering from digestive problems are given a nontoxic mixture containing barium before an X-ray. This mixture shows up clearly on X-rays allowing doctors to locate and diagnose the problem. Barium is also used in fluorescent lights to produce a perfect vacuum, removing all traces of gas, and in the coating on photographic paper.

### 88 RADIUM | Ra

The name comes from the Latin *radius,* meaning "ray," since radium glows faintly in the dark. It is a poisonous, heavy, radioactive metal with a longest half-life of 1,600 years. Radium is present in soils, which makes Earth a naturally radioactive planet. It is taken up by plants and also released into the environment through cement production and coal burning. It was used in the luminous paint on clock and watch dials, but it caused radiation sickness in many of the workers, mainly because they licked the bristle brushes to make a fine point for painting these dials.

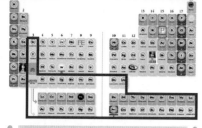

# LANTHANIDES

*Used to be known as rare earths, but not all are rare. They are silver, silvery-white, or gray metals. They share many common properties, which makes them difficult to separate.*

## LANTHANIDES

*Also called rare-earth metals, these are found in compound minerals containing most of the lanthanide elements. Many were found in Ytterby, Sweden.*

### 21 SCANDIUM — **Sc**

When it was discovered, this element was thought to exist only in Scandinavia. A lightweight and very expensive element, scandium is used to increase the striking power of baseball bats.

### 39 YTTRIUM — **Y**

Named after the Swedish village of Ytterby, where an odd piece of black rock containing yttrium and three other elements was found in 1787. It is used for making the red color in televisions.

### 57 LANTHANUM — **La**

The name comes from the Greek word *lanthanein*, meaning "to lie hidden." This element tarnishes in minutes and is used in lighting and glassmaking.

### 58 CERIUM — **Ce**

Cerium is named after the asteroid Ceres, and the Roman goddess of agriculture. It burns when heated and is used in self-cleaning ovens.

### 59 PRASEODYMIUM — **Pr**

A striking green color, this element's name comes from the Greek words *prasios didymos*, meaning "green twin." It is used in visor and goggle glass.

### 60 NEODYMIUM — **Nd**

Found with element 59, neodymium was named after the Greek words *neos didymos*, meaning "new twin." It makes powerful permanent magnets.

### 61 PROMETHIUM — **Pm**

Named after Prometheus, who stole fire from gods and gave it to humans.

### 62 SAMARIUM — **Sm**

This element was first extracted from the mineral samarskite and is named after it. When mixed with cobalt, it forms permanent magnets that do not lose their magnetism easily.

### 63 EUROPIUM — **Eu**

Named after Europe, europium is bright red and used in television tubes and fluorescent lights.

### 64 GADOLINIUM — **Gd**

Named after Swedish scientist Johan Gadolin, who investigated the first rare-earth minerals. Its magnetic properties allows it to be tracked through the body, so it is used for magnetic resonance imaging in medical diagnosis.

### 65 TERBIUM — **Tb**

This rare, silver-colored element is named after the Swedish village of Yt*terb*y, where the first example was found. It's used in X-ray imaging screens and CDs.

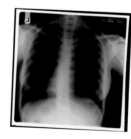

### 66 DYSPROSIUM — **Dy**

Named for the Greek word *dysprositos*, meaning "hard to get," this element was tricky to isolate.

### 67 HOLMIUM — **Ho**

Named from the Latin word for Stockholm, *Holmia*, holmium is used in laser surgery. Dyprosium and holmium have the highest magnetic strength of all the elements.

### 68 ERBIUM — **Er**

This is another element named from Yt*terb*y, Sweden. Erbium absorbs infrared rays so it is used in the glass of safety goggles for welders and glassblowers. It is also used to make the pink tint for glass in sunglasses, glassware, and jewelry.

### 69 THULIUM — **Tm**

Thule is an ancient name for Scandinavia. This element has few uses as it is rare and costly and cheaper elements can be substituted.

### 70 YTTERBIUM — **Yb**

Also named from Ytterby, Sweden, it's used in lasers and to improve stainless steel.

### 71 LUTETIUM — **Lu**

The name comes from Lutetia, the Roman name for Paris. This is the most expensive metal in the world.

# *and* Actinides

## ACTINIDES
*Most of these radioactive rare-earth metals are made in nuclear reactors.*

### 89 ACTINIUM (Ac)
The name comes from the Greek word *aktinos*, meaning "ray." It is so radioactive, it glows in the dark.

### 90 THORIUM (Th)
Named after Thor, the Scandinavian god of war, thorium is used to fuel nuclear reactors.

### 91 PROTACTINIUM (Pa)
This decays to form actinium. The name proactinium means "before actinium." It has no known uses.

### 92 URANIUM (U)
Uranium is named after the planet Uranus, and the Greek god of the heavens. This important element is used as the fuel in nuclear reactors to generate electricity.

### 93 NEPTUNIUM (Np)
Named after the planet Neptune, and the Greek god of the seas, neptunium is produced in the spent fuel rods in nuclear reactors. It is only weakly radioactive.

### 94 PLUTONIUM (Pu)
Named after the planet Pluto, this element is used to fuel nuclear reactors and in nuclear weapons. It was also used as a power source on the 1971 Apollo 14 lunar flight and for two Voyager spacecraft.

### 95 AMERICIUM (Am)
Named after America, this element's main use is in smoke detectors, where it puts out a tiny current. Smoke interferes with the current and sets off the alarm.

### 96 CURIUM (Cm)
It is named in honor of Pierre and Marie Curie. Curium is produced from plutonium and is used as a power source for pacemakers, navigational buoys, and spacecraft.

### 97 BERKELIUM (Bk)
The name is from Berkeley, California, where it was first made. Obtained from plutonium in nuclear reactors, less than 1 gram is made each year.

### 98 CALIFORNIUM (Cf)
Named for the University of California at Berkeley, where it was first made, this radioactive metal is made from plutonium in nuclear reactors. Only a few milligrams are made each year, mainly for use in cancer therapy.

### 99 EINSTEINIUM (Es)
This very rare metal was named after the physicist Albert Einstein.

### 100 FERMIUM (Fm)
Named after the nuclear physicist Enrico Fermi, it is made in millionths-of-a-gram quantities.

## TRANSFERMIUM ELEMENTS
*Elements with atomic number 101 and above have short half-lives, sometimes lasting only fractions of a second.*

### 101 MENDELEVIUM (Md)
Named after Dmitri Mendeleyev, creator of one of the first periodic tables.

### 102 NOBELIUM (No)
Named after Alfred Nobel, inventor of dynamite.

### 103 LAWRENCIUM (Lr)
It's named after Ernest Lawrence, inventor of the cyclotron, where radioactive elements are isolated.

### 104 RUTHERFORDIUM (Rf)
It's named after the physicist Ernest Rutherford, who was one of the first people to explain the structure of the atom.

### 105 DUBNIUM (Db)
It's named after the Russian town of Dubna, where it was first made.

### 106 SEABORGIUM (Sg)
This element is named after Glenn Seaborg, an American physicist.

### 107 BOHRIUM (Bh)
It's named after physicist Niels Bohr, who was first to correctly explain atomic structure.

### 108 HASSIUM (Hs)
It's named after German state of Hesse, home of the German Nuclear Research Institute.

### 109 MEITNERIUM (Mt)
It's named after the Austrian physicist Lise Meitner, who first suggested that radioactive atoms could spontaneously split apart releasing energy.

### 110 DARMSTADTIUM (Ds)
It's named after Darmstadt, Germany, where it was first made.

### 111 ROENTGENIUM (Rg)
Named and recognized as an element in 2004. Elements 112 onward are unrecognized, but their physical properties can be predicted from their group in the periodic table.

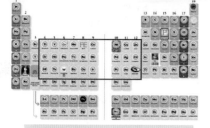

# *Transition* METALS

## 22 TITANIUM **Ti**

Titanium is named after the Titans, the sons of Uranus the sky god and Gaia the Earth goddess in Greek mythology. It is stronger than steel, but much lighter, so it is used for making aircraft engines, ships, and artificial joints.

## 40 ZIRCONIUM **Zr**

The name comes from the Persian word *zargon*, meaning "gold colored," because it forms gold-colored crystals. It is used in ceramics, knives, scissors, food packaging, and roll-on deodorant.

## 72 HAFNIUM **Hf**

The name comes from the Latin word for Copenhagen, *Hafnia*. A very high melting point and corrosion resistance make hafnium useful for nuclear reactors and submarine parts.

## 23 VANADIUM **V**

Vanadium is named after Vanadis, the Scandinavian goddess of beauty. It is a silvery metal that resists corrosion and is added to steel to strengthen it. The parts of the first Ford model T were made from vanadium steel.

## 41 NIOBIUM **Nb**

Named after Niobe, in Greek mythology the daughter of King Tantalus, since niobium has similar properties to tantalum. A silvery metal that is very resistant to corrosion, it is used in pipelines, aviation, and jewelry.

## 73 TANTALUM **Ta**

Tantalum is named after Tantalus, the legendary Greek king who was tormented in the underworld, as scientists were tormented trying to isolate it. It is used for missiles and aircraft.

## 24 CHROMIUM **Cr**

The name comes from the Greek word *chroma*, which means "color," because chromium salts are extremely colorful. It is used in tanning to make leather water-resistant, and added to steel to make stainless steel.

## 42 MOLYBDENUM **Mo**

The name comes from the Greek word *molybos*, meaning lead, because it was once mistaken for lead ore. It is used as a lubricant and as a steel alloy in car, aircraft, and rocket engine parts.

## 74 TUNGSTEN **W**

The name tungsten comes from the Swedish words *tung sten*, meaning "heavy stone." The symbol comes from its alternative name wolfram (wolf dirt) used by German tin miners, who disliked it. Tungsten has the highest melting point of all the metals, so is used for the filaments of lightbulbs and other types of lighting. It is alloyed with other metals to strengthen them.

## 25 MANGANESE **Mn**

This element's name comes from its mineral magnetite. Manganese improves strength, wear resistance, and rolling and forging properties of steel, so it is used in making railroad tracks, moving machinery, safes, helmets, and prison bars.

## 43 TECHNETIUM **T**

This was the first artificially made element, so it was named for the Greek word for artificial—*tekhnetos*. All the original technetium present when the Earth was formed has long since decayed. Today it is made in spent nuclear fuel rods. Highly radioactive, it is used in medical diagnosis.

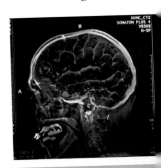

## 75 RHENIUM **Re**

This is named after *Rhenus*, the Latin name for the Rhine River. It has a very high melting point, second only to tungsten and is among the rarest metals on Earth. Rhenium is used in oven and lamp filaments measuring temperatures above 3,632°F (2,000°C).

## 26 IRON — Fe

The name comes from the Anglo Saxon word *iren*, but the symbol Fe is from the Latin name *ferrum*. Iron rusts easily, but with small amounts of carbon, it makes steel. Different types of steel have many uses, such as in construction, architecture, and jewelry.

## 44 RUTHENIUM — Ru

The name comes from *Ruthenia*, the Latin name for Russia. This element hardens platinum and palladium for electrical contacts and is extremely rare.

## 76 OSMIUM — Os

The name comes from the Greek *osme*, meaning "smell," because the metal surface gives off a strong odor. It is the densest of all the elements and as rare as gold. It was once used for pen nibs and in clock bearings. It's also used to detect fingerprints, revealing minute traces of oils left by a finger.

## 27 COBALT — Co

Cobalt is named from the German word *kobald*, meaning "goblin." It can be magnetized and so is used to make magnets. It makes a rich blue color used in ceramics and paints. In the 1700s, spies used it as an invisible ink, which revealed the messages when heated.

## 45 RHODIUM — Rh

Named for the Greek word *rhodon*, meaning "rose colored," rhodium is the rarest nonradioactive metal on Earth. It is an excellent reflector and used for coating mirrors and headlights.

## 77 IRIDIUM — Ir

This metal is named for Iris, Greek goddess of the rainbow, because its salts are multicolored. Iridium is one of the rarest metals and the most corrosion-resistant. It is used for deep water pipes and for the contacts in spark plugs.

## 28 NICKEL — Ni

Nickel is named after the German word *kupfernickel*, meaning "imp," because German copper miners found the reddish-brown ore had little use except for coloring glass green. Nickel resists corrosion at high temperatures and for this reason, it is used in gas turbines and rocket engines.

## 46 PALLADIUM — Pd

The name comes from Pallas, the Greek goddess of wisdom. Hydrogen gas can filter through it, so palladium is used to remove hydrocarbons from fuels.

## 78 PLATINUM — Pt

The name is derived from the Spanish word *platina*, meaning "little silver." Although it is almost as rare and expensive as gold, platinum is found in or has been used in the manufacture of one out of every five products we buy. It is part of the magnetic coating for computer hard disks for storing information.

## 29 COPPER — Cu

The name is from *cuprum*, the Latin name for Cyprus, as the island was a major exporter of copper in ancient times. Copper was the first metal to be worked, and the discovery that it could be hardened with tin to form the alloy bronze ushered in the Bronze Age. Copper conducts heat and electricity, so is used as wire, and it has been used for coinage since ancient times. The blood of octopus, snails, and spiders is blue because copper carries oxygen around their bodies.

## 47 SILVER — Ag

The name is from the Anglo-Saxon word *seolfor*, and the chemical symbol from the Latin *argentum*, both meaning "silver." Argentina was so-named in the hope that it was rich in silver. It has many uses due to its amazing conducting and reflective properties.

## 79 GOLD — Au

The name is the Anglo-Saxon word for yellow, and the symbol comes from the Latin *aurum*, meaning "dawn." It is the most malleable metal—one gram can be beaten into a sheet of 10 square feet (1 sq m). It is corrosion-resistant and is one of the few metals to occur in its natural state.

## 30 ZINC — Zn

From the German word *zink*, zinc is mixed with copper to make brass and covers other metals to prevent corrosion. Its compounds are used in rubber and plastics, X-ray screens, televisions, and fluorescent lighting. Zinc weatherproof sheeting has been used for roofs, especially in Paris, France.

## 48 CADMIUM — Cd

The name comes from the Latin word *cadmia*, the name for calamine ore, from which cadmium is refined. Once common in paints and screws, it was found to be poisonous so it is now used mostly in batteries.

## 80 MERCURY — Hg

Named after the planet Mercury and the Roman god of speed, the symbol is from the Latin *hydrargyrum*, meaning "liquid silver." It has limited uses today due to its toxicity.

# Poor metals and

## Group 13
*The boron group are only found as compounds in nature.*

### 5 BORON — B

Named from the Arabic word *buraq*, meaning "borax," because boron is mainly extracted from borax ore. Boron is a dark powder with a high melting point. It gives toughness and heat-resistant qualities to Pyrex glass and ceramic glazes for tiles and kitchen equipment. It's also added to glass fiber to reinforce plastics and building insulation. Boron is used in making flakes of shredded paper for simulating snow on film sets. Boron compounds go into the manufacture of detergents, insecticides, and fertilizers. It's also found in face powder, adding a luster and silky texture.

### 13 ALUMINUM — Al

Its name comes from *alumen*, the Latin name for the mineral alum. Aluminum does not rust, is light and tough, and is easy to recycle. Among its many hundreds of uses, aluminum goes into window frames, door handles, metal tubing, parts for boats, cars, motor engines, and aircraft, and food packaging, such as cooking foil and drink cans. It's a good conductor of electricity and reflector of heat and light, so aluminum is used for power cables, insulation, heat-reflecting blankets, and solar mirrors.

### 31 GALLIUM — Ga

Gallium is thought to be named from *Gallia*, the Latin word for France. It is a soft, silvery metal, which is similar to aluminum. Gallium is used to make light-emitting diodes (LEDs) for electronic displays and watches. As a semiconductor of electricity it is particularly useful in the production of supercomputers and cell phones.

### 49 INDIUM — In

Indium gets its name from the Latin word *indicum*, meaning "violet" or "indigo"—the color of the brightest lines in its atomic spectrum. This element is soft and silvery, and when a piece of it is bent, it gives off a high-pitched shriek. Indium foils are used to assess the activity inside nuclear reactors.

### 81 THALLIUM — Tl

Thallium takes its name from *thallos,* the Greek word for green plant shoot. It is a soft, gray metal, which tarnishes very easily. Although it once went into hair removers and rat poisons, thallium is now banned for general use because it's toxic. Today, it is a component of glass for refractive lenses and infrared detectors.

## Group 14
*The carbon group contains a mix of metals and nonmetals.*

### 6 CARBON — C

Named from the Latin word *carbo* for charcoal, carbon appears in many forms and is the most extracted element from the Earth's surface. Energy-providing fossil fuels are reduced carbon. Carbon fibers are stronger than steel and are used to reinforce plastics for sports equipment, or woven into protective clothing as they absorb poisonous gases. As diamonds, graphite, carbon black, coke, and charcoal, carbon has many uses.

### 14 SILICON — Si

Named from the Latin word *silex* or *silicis,* meaning flint, which was humans' first tool. From glass to silicones, silicon chips, quartz crystals, and silicates, silicon plays a very useful role in many aspects of our lives.

### 32 GERMANIUM — Ge

Named after Germany, germanium is a brittle, silvery-white semimetal. As a semiconductor of electricity, it was the first element to go into transistors. Today, it has been replaced in electronic devices, but it is still a component of glass for wide-angle camera lenses, and it is also used in infrared devices.

### 50 TIN — Sn

As an Anglo-Saxon word, tin has a chemical symbol derived from its Latin word *stannum*. This refers to a soft, pliable metal. As one of the oldest known metals, tin was familiar to many ancient civilizations and was added to copper to make bronze. Today, tin is used as a coating for steel to make tinplate, added to lead for solder, and added to silver and copper for dental amalgams. It is a component of pewter, metals for bells, and Babbitt metal in bearings.

# Nonmetals

## 82 LEAD — Pb

Widely used since Roman times, lead takes its name from the Anglo-Saxon word *laedan*. Its chemical symbol, from the Latin word *plumbium*, gave its name to the plumb line tool, which was a lead weight tied to the end of a string. Lead is a dull, silver-gray, soft, weak, but easily worked metal. Most of the traditional uses for lead, such as water pipes, house paint, and an additive in gasoline, are now banned as lead is poisonous. Today, its main uses are for making underground cable sheathing, car batteries, roof cladding, lead crystal, stained-glass windows, and sports weights. It is also used to protect people from radiation.

## Group 15

*The elements in the nitrogen group vary widely in physical appearance, but share some common chemical behavior.*

## 7 NITROGEN — N

Nitrogen was named from the Greek words *nitron* and *genes*, meaning "niter forming"; niter is the old name for saltpeter used in gunpowder and explosives. It is used in the chemical industry to make many chemical compounds that end up in our food, our clothes, our cars, our homes, and our medicines.

## 15 PHOSPHORUS — P

Named from the Greek word *phosphoros*, meaning "bringer of light," white phosphorus is dangerously flammable and a deadly poison. However, combined with oxygen, phosphate is essential to us and plants. Phosphates are stored in seeds for new plants to use when beginning to grow, so it is added to fertilizers. But if it is overused, too much phosphate enters lakes and rivers, causing excess growth of algae, which robs the water of oxygen for other plants and animals. Therefore, it is a legal requirement to remove phosphate from sewage and recycle it for farming and industrial uses. Phosphates are added to food, such as self-rising flour to make cakes, pastries, and biscuits rise, giving a lighter texture. Other uses include animal feed supplements, cleaning products, flame retardants, and coating metals to remove and prevent rust.

## 33 ARSENIC — As

Human contact with arsenic goes back over 5,000 years, but it was identified by Albertus Magnus in the 13th century. This element was probably given its name from *arsenikon*, the Greek name for the mineral yellow orpiment. This mineral, containing arsenic, was used by painters to make a bright yellow color that unfortunately faded dramatically over time and came away from the canvas. In the 19th century, arsenic was used in the manufacture of green and blue wallpaper, which, if damp, gave off a toxic gas that would cause death from arsenic poisoning. Now arsenic is only used in the production of special types of glass, as a wood preservative, and as a semiconductor that can convert electric current to laser light.

## 51 ANTIMONY — Sb

Familiar to ancient civilizations, but identified by an unknown alchemist during the Middle Ages, antimony is named from the Greek words *anti* and *monos*, meaning "not alone." Its chemical symbol comes from the Latin word *stibium*, which was the name of its compound known in ancient times. As a gray powder, antimony expands as it becomes a brittle, silvery, hard solid. Antimony is used in the printing industry, and in the production of batteries, bearings, and cable sheathing. It is added to plastics as a flame retardant, especially in car components, televisions, and crib mattresses.

## 83 BISMUTH — Bi

Bismuth gets its name from the German description *weisse Masse*, meaning "white mass," which in Latin is *bisemutum*. This metal is heavy, silvery, pink-tinged, and very brittle. Because it has a relatively low melting point, bismuth was once used to make electric fuses, and it is still a component of fire-sprinkler systems. It's used in medicines for indigestion, and in cosmetics to give a pearly luster.

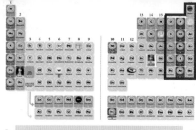

# Halogens and

## GROUP 16

*The elements in this group are sometimes called the chalcogens, meaning "pyrites forming," because some of these elements are found in metal ores.*

### 8 OXYGEN — O

The word oxygen comes from the ancient Greek words *oxys* and *genes*, meaning "acid forming." It is the most common element on Earth, making up half the weight of a human body. 110 million tons (100 million metric tons) is extracted from the air each year, mostly for use in steel making and the chemical industry.

### 16 SULFUR — S

The name comes from the Latin *sulfurium*, or the Sanskrit *sulvere*, both of which mean "sulfur." It burns if ignited, giving off the gas sulfur dioxide, which is used to make sulfuric acid, gunpowder, and fireworks.

### 34 SELENIUM — Se

The name is from the Greek word *selene*, meaning "moon." Selenium can exist in two forms: as a silvery metal or as a red powder. It conducts electricity very well and so it is used in photoelectric cells, photocopiers, solar cells, light meters, and semiconductors. Other uses include making ruby-colored glass and light-blocking glass. It is essential for humans, and our bodies contain about 14 milligrams. It is effective in blocking the effects of heavy metals such as arsenic, thallium, and the mercury found in fish.

### 52 TELLURIUM — Te

This semimetallic gray powder was named for the Latin word *tellus*, meaning "Earth." Its compounds are poisonous and eating them causes very unpleasant body odors and bad breath. It is added to copper and stainless steel to harden them and improve their ability to be machined. It is also added to lead to make it harder and more acid-resistant for use in batteries.

### 84 POLONIUM — Po

Discovered by the chemist Marie Curie in 1898, this radioactive element takes its name from Poland, her homeland. Marie Curie isolated polonium from the uranium ore pitchblende, in which it exists in tiny amounts. It is produced today in gram quantities from bismuth in nuclear reactors, and used as a source of alpha radiation or as a heat source in space vehicles. At one time, polonium was used in textile mills and in the manufacture of photographic plates. In 2006, the element gained international notoriety when it was used for the mysterious fatal poisoning of the Russian dissident Alexander Litvinenko, in London.

## GROUP 17

*The name of the gases in this group, halogens, comes from the Greek words* hals *and* genes, *meaning "salt-forming." Compounds containing halogens are called salts.*

### 9 FLUORINE — F

The name comes from the Latin word *fleure*, meaning "flow." Fluorine salts, known as fluorides, were used for centuries in welding metals and for frosting glass before the element itself was isolated. Today, fluorine is used in the nuclear power industry, in an insulating gas used in high-power electricity transformers, and to treat plastics used as fuel tanks to prevent fluids from leaking. Fluoride is added to drinking water and toothpaste to help prevent tooth decay. Fluorine gas quickly attacks all metals—steel wool bursts into flames when exposed to it.

### 17 CHLORINE — Cl

The name of this element comes from the Greek word *chloros*, which means "pale green," because this element is a dense green gas with a choking smell. It is very poisonous and was used as a weapon during World War I. The gas is made from salt (sodium chloride) and is used in the manufacture of bleach, to bleach wood pulp for paper manufacture, to purify drinking water, and to disinfect swimming pools. Chlorine is the C in PVC plastic.

# NOBLE *gases*

## 35 BROMINE — Br

From the Greek *bromos*, meaning "stench," this is a deep-red, oily liquid with a very unpleasant smell. It is poisonous and the liquid burns skin. It is extracted from natural brines and seawater and is used to make fuels and additives, insecticides, fire extinguishers, and pharmaceuticals. The use of bromide salts as flame-retardants and as sedatives has been discontinued because the compounds are slightly toxic and can mimic hormones.

## 53 IODINE — I

The name comes from the Greek word *iodes*, meaning "violet," because iodine turns into a violet-colored gas when it is heated. Iodine is used in the pharmaceutical industry as an antiseptic, in animal feed, in printing inks and dyes, in industrial catalysts, and in photographic chemicals. Iodine vapor was important in the development of the first photographs.

## 85 ASTATINE — At

The name is from the Greek word *astatos*, meaning "unstable." This element doesn't exist outside nuclear facilities or research labs.

## GROUP 18

*These noble gases are the colorless, odorless gases that are mostly inert, which means they don't join up or react with any other element. They are also called rare or inert gases and exist as individual atoms, rather than molecules.*

## 2 HELIUM — He

Named for the Greek word *helios*, meaning "Sun," as helium is one of the main components of the Sun. It is extracted from natural gas wells for use in low-temperature instruments, lasers, welding, deep-sea diving, and powering rockets.

## 10 NEON — Ne

Named for the Greek word *neo*, meaning "new," neon is a colorless, odorless gas that exists in small quantities in air. It is the second-lightest noble gas and does not react with any other substance. It is produced from liquid air for use in ornamental lighting because it glows red when an electrical discharge is passed through it. These neon signs will last up to 20 years, and red signs are made only from neon.

## 18 ARGON — Ar

The name argon is from the Greek *argo*, meaning "inactive." This is the third most abundant gas, making up one percent of the atmosphere. Argon is used inside lightbulbs because it does not react with the filament even at high temperatures. Blue argon lasers are used in surgery to join arteries, destroy tumors, and correct eye defects. Argon gas is used to protect old materials or documents, which would be destroyed in air.

## 36 KRYPTON — Kr

The name of this element is taken from the Greek word *kryptos*, meaning "hidden," because it was very difficult to discover. Krypton is a colorless, odorless gas that does not react with anything except for fluorine gas. One type of krypton has a line in its atomic spectrum that was used for 23 years as the standard measure of length: 1 meter was defined as exactly 1,650,763.73 wavelengths of this line. Krypton is one of the rarest gases in the Earth's atmosphere, accounting for only 1 part per million by volume.

*The planet Krypton and kryptonite are made up.*

## 54 XENON — Xe

The name comes from the Greek word *xenos*, meaning "stranger." Xenon emits a blue glow when excited by electricity and so is used for strobe lighting, sunbeds, fog lights, road signs, and germ-killing food lamps. Xenon powers the engines used in space vehicles.

## 86 RADON — Rn

Radon is produced by the element radium as it decays. It is colorless and odorless and is chemically inert, but it is dangerous because it gives off radiation. There is a detectable amount in the atmosphere, and concentrations can build up indoors in certain areas. Radon accumulates in underground caves and mines. Some spas in Japan and Austria specialize in radon "bathing," which supposedly makes people feel young and energetic.

93

# GLOSSARY

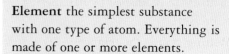

**Actinides** heavy radioactive elements with atomic numbers 89 to 103.

**Alchemy** the quest for turning metals into gold, for curing all diseases, and for becoming immortal.

**Alkali metals** the very reactive silvery metals in Group 1 on the periodic table.

**Alkaline earth metals** the reactive, soft, silvery metals in Group 2 on the periodic table.

**Alloy** a mixture of two or more metals.

**Atom** a tiny particle of an element, consisting of a central nucleus surrounded by one or more electrons.

**Atomic number** the number of protons inside the nucleus of an atom. A neutral atom has the same number of orbiting electrons.

**Atomic spectrum** the radiation given off by an atom when excited by electricity or heat.

**Atomic structure** the model of an atom, showing the position of the protons, neutrons, and electrons.

**Atomic weight** the average weight of the atoms of an element as they exist in their natural form on Earth.

**Boiling point** the temperature at which a liquid turns into a gas at a specified air pressure.

**Bond** when two atoms join together either by sharing electrons in their outer orbit, or by losing or gaining electrons in their outer orbit.

**Compound** two or more elements strongly joined together.

**Charge (or electric charge)** an electrical imbalance in an atom caused by the loss or addition of electrons. It can be either negative (gain of electron or electrons) or positive (loss of electron or electrons).

**Chemical formula** a sequence of symbols showing the number and kinds of atoms in a molecule or compound.

**Chemical properties** an element's behavior during chemical reactions.

**Chemical reaction** the change or transformation of the way atoms are grouped together, making a new compound or compounds.

**Chemical symbols** a single capital letter or a combination of a capital letter and a small one used to represent an atom of an element. These are used to write chemical formulas.

**Chemistry** the scientific study of the properties and reactions of the elements.

**Combustion** a process where substances are burned in oxygen.

**Conductor** an element that transmits heat, sound, or electricity very well.

**Corrosion** a process where metals or alloys crumble away, especially when in contact with water and oxygen.

**Dissolve** to add a solid to a liquid to form a liquid solution.

**Electric circuit** the path along which an electric charge can flow.

**Electrolysis** the process of breaking up compounds using electricity.

**Electron** one of the three main particles in an atom (with the proton and neutron). It moves around the nucleus of an atom and has a negative charge. The number of electrons in an atom's outer orbits affects the properties of the element.

**Element** the simplest substance with one type of atom. Everything is made of one or more elements.

**Evaporate** to draw out moisture by heating, leaving behind any dry solids.

**Experiment** the process of doing something under controlled conditions to discover something or prove something.

**Flame-retardant** a compound that prevents a flammable material from catching fire or at least slows down the burning.

**Flammable** to burst into flame easily.

**Fluorescent** to glow when exposed to radiation.

**Freezing point** the temperature at which a liquid changes into a solid.

**Gas** a state in which an element's atoms are far apart and move around randomly and quickly.

**Halogens** the nonmetallic elements in Group 17 of the periodic table.

**Inert** the behavior of an element unwilling to take part in a chemical reaction with other elements.

**Insulator** an element that is poor at conducting heat, sound, or electricity.

**Lanthanides** metallic elements with atomic numbers 57 to 71.

**Liquid** a state between a solid and a gas, in which an element's atoms can slide around but remain close together and attract one another.

**Magnetic** the property of some elements, especially iron, to attract or repel similar materials.

**Malleable** the property of some elements to be shaped by hammering or pressure.

**Melting point** the temperature at which a solid turns into a liquid.

**Metal** an element that is a solid, often with a shiny surface, is a good conductor of heat and light, and can be molded into shapes without breaking.

**Mineral** a natural solid extracted from the ground. It contains one or more elements.

**Molecule** a single particle of a compound. Its two or more atoms are strongly joined together.

**Nanotechnology** the scientific method of working with materials at the scale of their atoms and molecules.

**Neutron** one of the two main particles in the nucleus of an atom. It has no electric charge.

**Noble gas** the mostly inert, colorless gases in Group 18 on the periodic table.

**Nonmetal** an element that is brittle in its solid form and is a poorer conductor of heat, electricity, and light than metals.

**Nuclear reactor** a device where neutrons are bombarded at the nucleus of certain atoms, causing them to split and release further neutrons, generating heat and making new radioactive elements.

**Nucleus** the solid center of an atom, made up of protons and neutrons.

**Ore** a mineral from which an element, especially a metal, is extracted.

**Oxides** the compounds made when metals join with oxygen.

**Particles** basic units from which all substances are made, such as atoms or molecules. Subatomic particles are those smaller than an atom, such as protons.

**Periodic table** a diagram classifying all the known elements.

**Philosophers' stone** the substance that alchemists believed would change metals into gold and give immortality.

**Phosphors** materials that glow with a visible light when hit by electrons.

**Physical properties** features of an element that can be measured and seen without any chemical reactions.

**Properties** an element's physical features and its behavior with other elements and during chemical reactions.

**Proton** one of the two main particles found in the nucleus of atoms. It has a positive charge.

**Radiation** high-speed energy traveling as invisible particles (electromagnetic radiation) or rays given off by radioactive elements.

**Radioactive** the property of an element with an unstable nucleus that releases high-speed particles or rays as its nucleus breaks down, trying to stabilize.

**Radioactive decay** the conversion of one radioactive element into another radioactive element over time. The half-life is the time taken for half of a sample of a radioactive element to turn into other elements.

**Reactive** the behavior of an element eager to take part in a chemical reaction.

**Reflector** an element that throws back light and shows an image on its shiny surface.

**Resistant** the property of an element that prevents heat, light, water, or something else from affecting it.

**Salt** a crystallized solid formed when a metal bonds with a nonmetal.

**Semiconductor** an element that is partly good at transmitting heat, sound, or electricity in some situations.

**Solid** a state in which an element's atoms are joined together in a rigid structure.

**Sterilize** to remove bacteria and other microorganisms from a substance.

**Tarnish** to discolor, especially when in air or dirt.

**Temperature** measure of how hot or cold something is.

**Toxic** a substance able to kill people.

**Transition metals** the metals in Groups 3 to 12 of the periodic table. Most of these are strong, have high melting and boiling points, and are good conductors.

**Vacuum** an enclosed space with no or very little gas.

**X-ray** a form of invisible radiation. X-rays pass through most parts of the human body, but not bones or teeth.

# INDEX

## Acknowledgments

Dorling Kindersley would like to thank the following people for help with this book: Lisa Magloff, Fleur Star, Myriam Megharbi, Martin Copeland.

The publisher would like to thank the following for their kind permission to reproduce their photographs:

(Key: a-above; b-below/bottom; c-center; f-far; l-left; r-right; t-top)

Alamy Images: 69bl; Mick Broughton 45l; Bruce Coleman Inc. / Edward R. Degginger 44clb, 69ftr; Classic Image 17br; Kathy de Witt 55tr; Digital Archive Japan 26cla; flash bang wallop 68bl; Foodfolio 28c; D. Hurst 55cra; ImageState / Pictor International 12tc, 27cl, 76tc, 76tl, 77bl, 77br, 82bc, 96bc, 96bl; Imagina Photography(www.imagina.bc.ca) / Atsushi Tsunoda 89; Imagina Photography (www.imagina.bc.ca) / Tsunoda 8-9; JG Photography 78-79; Emmanuel Lattes 73cla; Gareth McCormack 69bl (background); Ian Miles / Flashpoint Pictures 78br; Charlie Newham 7br; Pictorial Press Ltd 14br; The Print Collector 49clb; Mark Sykes 63 (background); Travelshots 54clb; Ardea: John Daniels 28br, 42bl, 42-43c; The Art Archive: British Library, London 12c; The Bridgeman Art Library: Derby Museum and Art Gallery, UK 15br; Corbis: Yann Arthus-Bertrand 39bl; Bettmann 3bl, 11br, 12bl, 19br, 68tr, 76bl, 77c; Blue Lantern Studio 68tc; Lee Cohen 32br; Chris Collins 50c; Nathalie Darbellay / Sygma 14-15t; Tim Davis 74br; Digital Art 32-33, 80-81b; Jose Fuste Raga 6b; Gunter Marx Photography 75bl; H et M / photocuisine 75br; Lindsay Herbberd 49cla; Matthias Kulka 40t; Matthias Kulka / zefa 45tr; Mark M. Lawrence 72cl; NASA 33cr, 36t; Charles O'Rear 67tc, 72bl; Roger Ressmeyer / NASA 28tc, 31tr; Reuters 69tc; Guenter Rossenbach / zefa 28tl, 54-55b; Stapleton Collection 11cr, 15c; Les Stone / Zuma 73clb; Hein van den Heuvel / zefa 49tr; Josh Westrich / zefa 67r; Nik Wheeler 49c; Douglas Whyte 70-71; Zefa 51tl, 58c; DK Images: Anglo-Australian Observatory 6-7t (background); British Museum 11crb, 48cra, 60bc, 60cra, 60tc, 60tr, 62cb, 63bc, 63bl, 63br, 63crb, 63fbr, 63fcr, 89tl; Egyptian Museum, Cairo 62cra; Football Museum, Preston 63cra; IFREMER, Paris 88bl; Jamie Marshall 49tl; Judith Miller / Fellows & Sons 89tc (ring); Judith Miller / Antique Glass - Frank Dux Antiques 69tr; Judith Miller / Biblion 69bc; Judith Miller / Keller & Ross 89bl; Judith Miller / Wallis and Wallis 93br; National Motor Museum, Beaulieu 1tl (car); Natural History Museum, London 44cl; Stephen Oliver 41br, 81fbl, 95; Oxford University Museum of Natural History 44cla; Pitt Rivers Museum, University of Oxford 8tl; Rough Guides 89tc, 91tr; Science Museum, London 20cl, 25tr, 45tc; Getty Images: Scott Andrews 35ca, 82l; Barry Austin Photography / Riser 78bc; Gary S. Chapman / Photographer's Choice 32-33c; Peter Dazeley 83br, 96tl; Peter Dazeley / The Image Bank 61cra; Discovery Channel Images / Jeff Foott 79bl; Jeremy Frechette / The Image Bank 61c; Photographer's Choice / Victoria Blackie 81crb; Antonio M. Rosario 11c; Nicolas Russell 35t; Craig van der Lende / The Image Bank 17cr; naturepl.com: Neil Lucas 74bl; Science Photo Library: 10tl, 13br, 16b, 16c, 16t, 16-17c, 17tr, 18bl, 18tl, 21bl, 21br, 22tr, 34bl, 39c, 39tl, 42cl, 46crb, 58tc, 78cl; Andrew Lambert Photography 45ca, 66tr; George Bernard 60cl; Ken Biggs 63 (circuit board); Martyn F. Chillmaid 17cla; Lynette Cook 36b; Kevin Curtis 89tr; Roberto De Gugliemo 32cl; Mark Garlick 30tc, 30tl, 31tc; Pascal Goetgheluck 60c, 81br; Klaus Guldbrandsen 23br, 39tr, 82br; Coneyl Jay 84cb; Ben Johnson 71br; James King-Holmes 41cb, 84c; Ton Kinsbergen 86bl; Mehau Kulyk 54cl; Russ Lappa 56 (titanium), 57 (cobalt); Leonard Lessin 84bl; Dr P. Marazzi 61tr; George Mattei 88cr; Astrid & Hanns-Frieder Michler 23cl; NASA 31cl; Susumu Nishinaga 28cr, 54tr; Omikron 25br; David Parker 67bc, 87tr; Alfred Pasieka 67c; Photo Researchers 22tl, 75cra; C. Powell, P. Fowler & D. Perkins 22-23; Philippe Psaila 35br; Gary Retherford 13bl; J.C. Revy 57crb; Ria Novosti 21tl, 23cr, 87br; Alexis Rosenfeld 35bl; Bill Sanderson 5t, 8cl; John Sanford 34tr, 82tr, 94tr; Mark A. Schneider 22bc, 22bl, 22br; Josh Sher 84cb; Sinclair Stammers 50t; Michael Szoenyi 87bl, 89ca; TEK Image 54cra; Sheila Terry 8tr, 14tl, 18br; Rich Treptow 57 (cadmium); Alexander Tsiaras 86tr; US Library Of Congress 27br; Dr Keith Wheeler 28cb, 73tc; Charles D. Winters 43c, 47bl, 56 (selenium)

JACKET IMAGES: Front: DK Images: National Motor Museum, Beaulieu tl (car)

All other images © Dorling Kindersley
For further information see: www.dkimages.com